T0245569

Praise for *Big Goals*

"Entrepreneurs with big dreams and ambitions will always benefit from working with the science of goal setting. Caroline has the unique ability of interpreting the science of goal setting in a relatable and actionable way."

—Dr. Nadine Hachach-Haram
Founder and CEO of Proximie

"As a founding CEO, I know how hard it is to take the right risks and have the grit it takes to see them through, two topics that Caroline Adams Miller explains in *Big Goals* with the most cutting-edge science available."

—Susan Tynan
CEO of Framebridge

"Caroline Adams Miller is the first person who has disrupted and updated the field of goal setting to make it understandable and relevant to everyone, regardless of age, race, or gender. This book is must reading for anyone who wants to accomplish their own Big Goal!"

—Dr. Lea Waters
CEO Visible Wellbeing,
Professorial Fellow The University of Melbourne

"No one is more dedicated to understanding and harnessing character strengths to live with intention and excellence than Caroline Adams Miller. Her unrelenting passion for discovering, translating, and sharing the best science to catalyze human flourishing makes her a beacon of excellence in the field. In her latest work, Caroline skillfully guides readers to achieve their most challenging goals, beautifully weaving the science of character strengths into the very fabric of goal setting, purpose, vision, and meaningful relationships."

—Dr. Jillian Coppley
President and Chief Programs and Services Officer,
VIA Institute on Character

"What makes Caroline Adams Miller and this book a stand-out is that she combines the facts with the psychology. Each is important but together, you can reach the stars. Reaching big goals isn't easy. In this book, though, anyone can access Caroline's extraordinary coaching to get you to where you want to go in life, better, faster. Caroline's approach is being adopted by our team and incorporated into GWI's own programs to ensure the next generation learns these essential lessons early on."

—Jennifer Openshaw
Chairman & CEO of Girls
With Impact and Author of The Millionaire Zone

"Caroline Adams Miller doesn't just talk a big game when she promises practical strategies for accomplishing our big goals; she delivers in her book, *Big Goals*. Drawing from a diverse group of researchers, Caroline generously brings us the most up-to-date and comprehensive guide on goal setting theory and her brand-new BRIDGE methodology, which when combined make it almost impossible NOT to be successful.. If you are looking for a book that empowers, encourages, and motivates you to set big goals *and* achieve them, this is the only playbook you will ever need."

—Wendy Conklin
The Chair Stylist & CEO of Chair Whimsy

"Who knew we were going about our goals all wrong? Caroline Adams Miller did, and thankfully she shares her science-backed ways to go after our goals *the right way*. Prepare for life-altering results after reading this book!"

—Jodi Wellman
Author of You Only Die Once

BiG
GOALS

CAROLINE ADAMS MILLER, MAPP

BiG
GOALS

The Science of Setting Them, Achieving Them, and Creating Your Best Life

FOREWORD BY BRIAN JOHNSON
CO-FOUNDER & CEO, HEROIC AND AUTHOR OF *ARETÉ*

WILEY

Published by John Wiley & Sons, Inc., Hoboken, New Jersey.
Published simultaneously in Canada.

For general information on our other products and services or for technical support, please contact our Customer Care Department within the United States at (800) 762-2974, outside the United States at (317) 572-3993 or fax (317) 572-4002.

Wiley also publishes its books in a variety of electronic formats. Some content that appears in print may not be available in electronic formats. For more information about Wiley products, visit our website at www.wiley.com.

Library of Congress Cataloging-in-Publication Data

Names: Miller, Caroline Adams, 1961- author
Title: Big goals : the science of setting them, achieving them, and creating your best life / Caroline Adams Miller.
Description: Hoboken, New Jersey : Wiley, [2025] | Includes index.
Identifiers: LCCN 2024031219 (print) | LCCN 2024031220 (ebook) | ISBN 9781394273317 (hardback) | ISBN 9781394273331 (adobe pdf) | ISBN 9781394273324 (epub)
Subjects: LCSH: Goal (Psychology) | Success. | Self-actualization (Psychology)
Classification: LCC BF505.G6 M53 2025 (print) | LCC BF505.G6 (ebook) | DDC 158.1—dc23/eng/20240801
LC record available at https://lccn.loc.gov/2024031219
LC ebook record available at https://lccn.loc.gov/2024031220

Cover Design: Paul McCarthy
SKY10092920_120424

To my grandson, Wally Miller: May you and all future grandchildren of mine be blessed with the strength of bold vision, the courage to test your limits, and the willingness to help make other people's dreams come true, too. Never forget that you can't keep what you don't give away.

Contents

Foreword

I've spent the better part of the last 25 years integrating ancient wisdom and modern science into practical tools to help people forge excellence and activate their Heroic potential.

During that time, I've studied Socrates in Athens, Jesus in Jerusalem, and Marcus Aurelius near the Danube of Hungary while reading more than 1,000 self-development books – including all the classics on goal setting and Positive Psychology.

In the process of distilling all that wisdom into a practical framework, I discovered Caroline Adams Miller and her work, including her pioneering book on the science of happiness and its intersection with the science of goal setting, *Creating Your Best Life*, and later *Getting Grit*, both of which I use in my work with Heroic coaches all over the world who are bringing areté and excellence to as many people as we can reach.

Caroline immediately became one of my all-time favorite Applied Positive Psychologists. In fact, she's at least tied for first as my all-time favorite PRACTICAL Applied Positive Psychologist!

Caroline has a gift for bringing the empirical wisdom from academia alive in the pages of her books – which is why I was so excited when she told me she was writing an updated book on the science of goal setting for the mass market that anyone from a high school student to a CEO could read and implement immediately.

Somehow, over the last several decades, no one has ever taken the time to write a book on THE most scientifically rigorous approach to setting goals.

Enter: *Big Goals: The Science of Setting Them, Achieving Them, and Creating Your Best Life*.

In this amazing book, Caroline walks us through the groundbreaking research by Edwin A. Locke and Gary P. Latham that led to their empirically proven "Goal Setting Theory," then she brilliantly extends their seminal ideas with her own "BRIDGE" framework to help us get from where we are to where we want to be. She has merged the best of ancient wisdom with the latest cutting-edge findings to give us all the best possible approach to setting, pursuing, and achieving any goal, but especially the big goals that we dream about, and that change us and the world around us for the better.

To put it bluntly: This is the only book on goal setting you'll ever need to buy. Period.

Brian Johnson
co-founder and CEO,
Heroic, and author of *Areté*

Introduction

"How many of you set big goals?" I always ask this question whenever I'm working with students at Wharton's Executive Education program, in global corporate settings, or delivering keynotes that span industries ranging from law to gaming. Almost everyone raises their hand.

"How many of you use Locke and Latham's goal setting theory to help you achieve those goals?" In response to that question, I've rarely seen more than two hands, if that, go up in a room.

I'm no longer surprised.

In 2005, I considered myself a goal setting expert and was working as an executive coach, speaker, and author helping others map out change in their lives and organizations. As a credentialed graduate of one of the top coach training programs in the world, I owned and had read every popular book I could find on goal setting and success. My professional certification from the International Coach Federation required that my client work include accurate goal setting processes that incorporated progress metrics and accountability. It helped that as the grandniece of Olympic gold, silver, and bronze medalists, I took the job of helping people to become their best selves and accomplish their hardest goals very seriously. I was trained, certified, and well-read on the topic. What could possibly be missing from my approach?

The answer is everything.

I Knew Nothing About Accurate Goal Setting

The scales about my lack of real knowledge around goals fell from my eyes in October 2005 when my homework in the Masters of Applied Positive Psychology (MAPP) program at the University of Pennsylvania included a research paper by Edwin Locke and Gary Latham, co-founders of goal setting theory (GST). I remember saying aloud in wonderment, "There's such a thing as goal setting theory that's based on research? There's a real science to achieving goals that I've never heard of or been taught?"

The moment I found out that GST was one of the most robust, evidence-based theories on motivation and that there were hundreds, if not thousands, of studies proving its efficacy and replicating findings that had been accumulating since 1960, I arranged to have the entire handbook of their theory loaned to me by Drexel University, which I promptly copied, one page at a time. I felt like I'd just been given the keys to the kingdom, and I was determined to learn as much as I could so that I could pass it along to clients and others who wanted to know the most effective, proven ways to accomplish their goals, too.

I subsequently discarded every book I had once revered on how to achieve success by such motivational authors as Steven Covey and Brian Tracy. None of them had a shred of evidence or science referenced in their writings, and there were zero sources cited. Furthermore, none of them mentioned GST or Locke and Latham, the two individuals who were clearly the foremost authorities in the world on the topic. As my year in the MAPP program progressed, I continued to learn about how to thrive, succeed, and maximize one's chances of achieving meaningful goals with concepts like self-regulation, emotional contagion, self-efficacy, priming, character strengths, and resilience – relevant research that had mostly been kept hidden in the Ivory Towers of academia where people like me in the "real world" couldn't access or use it.

After consulting with my mentor, Dr. Martin Seligman, the "father of Positive Psychology" and the creator of the MAPP program, we agreed that my Capstone project would be a start toward rectifying this problem. I wove together what I learned that year along with reams of other science on motivation, change, and well-being into a manuscript that ultimately became the world's first evidence-based guide to goal accomplishment for the mass market, and the first to map the brand-new research linking the science of happiness with the science of success. *Creating Your Best Life* (Sterling) hit the market in early 2009 in multiple languages, instantly becoming a classic among athletes, leaders in organizations, executive coaches, adults in midlife transition, and students crafting their future paths. It was reissued in 2021, and I was especially honored to see it continuing to ride the top of recommended reading lists as a top goal setting pick throughout the coronavirus pandemic, a period when many people started to question their career and life choices and seek a framework to create positive change for themselves.

The Science Remains Unknown

Fifteen years after *Creating Your Best Life* debuted, I feel more urgency than ever about the need to educate the world about the science of goal accomplishment, but in a shorter and more streamlined way. That is the book you are holding in your hands. I wrote it so that anyone from a manager in a Silicon Valley company to a middle school student can quickly grasp the concepts of goal setting science, walk through the steps from start to finish, and stand a good chance of becoming successful, or, at the very least, understanding what they need to do to make things happen **for** them and not **to** them.

My executive coaching clients are now exclusively CEOs who run organizations that are putting people in space, renovating outdoor environments, and disrupting educational, artistic, and financial industries. I still find that I'm the first person to ever teach them goal setting theory, which they then use to overhaul their company's approach to change. Most fly to my strategy offsite center in Rehoboth Beach, Delaware from all over the world once or twice a year to do in-depth strategy sessions so that they and their employees can benefit from having leaders who know the difference between learning goals and performance goals (Locke and Latham's definitions of these goals, not how some popular websites define them). Starting this annual process correctly reduces disengagement, enhances curiosity, results in greater success, and avoids the perils of what I call "goals gone wild" – situations in which performance and learning goals are reversed, often resulting in failure, a company's reputation loss, and even death in the worst cases.

Faux Excellence and Diseases of Despair

In the past decade, anxiety, depression, and suicide have continued to rise among teens and young adults. COVID-19 and the forced separation of children from their friends through remote learning only accelerated these trends and added to the mental health problems that had been brewing for years. Part of those challenges came from the society that Generation X had created for their children. When I wrote *Getting Grit* (2017) I covered the rise in the "Self-Esteem Parenting" movement which began in the 1990s and preached that making children happy at all costs and giving them what they wanted without struggle would raise their self-confidence and result in a positive work ethic. Neither happened. Instead, it gave rise to the "everyone is a winner" mentality and rampant grade inflation that continue to this day.

> A December 2023 report by Ray C. Fair, an economics professor at Yale, said that close to 80% of Yale University students received A's for their work, numbers matched by Harvard and other private schools. Public schools trail only slightly in overall GPA averages. University officials feel powerless to change the relentless upward trajectory of *faux* excellence, which spiked sharply during the pandemic, and which they say is exerting even more pressure on students, not less. Amanda Claybaugh, dean of Harvard's undergraduate education, explained, "Students feel the need to distinguish themselves outside the classroom because they are essentially indistinguishable inside the classroom. Extracurriculars, which should be stress relieving, become stress producing."

Throughout childhood, Millennials were often not exposed by schools, sports teams, or society to traditional exemplars of high achievement or expectations to do hard things that required resilience, willpower, or curiosity. Gatekeepers didn't want to discourage or stress them, and competition was considered by many authority figures to be unfair.

Is it any wonder that a generation raised on limited expectations of excellence might find themselves ill-equipped to handle experiences of disappointment, relationship rejection, and honest performance reviews in the workplace? When we believe people are too fragile to deal with stress and live in a world filled with images of Instagram perfection and YouTube moments of fame that they have no idea how to achieve, it's no wonder they might become depressed or anxious when staring at their future. A lifetime of getting automatic accolades for standard efforts and accumulating participation trophies simply for being on any team in a soccer league has left many unable – or unwilling – to turn their own dreams into reality. They need a new approach and tools to help them bridge their current position to a more empowered future.

> Rates of depression and anxiety among US adolescents were mostly constant during the 2,000s, but many studies show that those numbers rose by more than 50% from 2010 to 2019, which coincides with the arrival and spread of the smartphone in 2008. Gallup notes that screen time among teens has skyrocketed, with 4.8 hours a day mostly going toward social media apps like TikTok, Instagram, and Snapchat, with girls logging up to 5.3 hours daily. Excessive screen time has been linked to procrastination and an inability to focus on one's goals, something three-quarters of college students say is chronic and problematic, wreaking havoc on their mental health, relationships, and work. Adding to their challenges, rates of post-traumatic stress disorder (PTSD) among college students more than doubled between 2017 and 2022, surprising one of the researchers who called the findings "indeed shocking."

In recent years economists have also been discussing the rise in "diseases of despair," conditions that are particularly pronounced in women at midlife who don't feel their lives have purpose or meaning. Although there are many factors that contribute to the spike in eating disorders, depression, opioid abuse, alcoholism, and unhappiness seen in this age group, it's thought that lacking the tools to identify and successfully pursue their own goals is also part of the problems besetting women. I firmly believe that goal setting science isn't just an important means to help address the problems we see among our youth and young adults, I also think it can be a positive addition to how women – and men – handle the relationship, job, physical, and mental changes that occur at midlife, a period also correlated with the lowest levels of happiness in life.

Learned Mastery, Not Learned Helplessness

Seligman, who became a treasured friend and mentor at Penn, is renowned for the decades he spent in psychology studying depression and other ills prior to pioneering the field of Positive Psychology in 2,000, which is the study of flourishing individuals, organizations, and countries. He is perhaps best known known for his theory of "learned helplessness," which posited that dogs in cages given electrical shocks and prevented from escaping, and who then lay down and gave up even when their cages were left open, had learned to be "helpless."

Entire cities, educational programs, and social services were promulgated based on this theory so that individuals wouldn't give up when they had the equivalent of electrical shocks. "Learned helplessness" is still such a common phrase that rarely a week goes by without someone saying to me that they or someone else has been the victim of "learned helplessness," and that giving up on something had been the natural consequence of being repeatedly stymied in their goal pursuit.

We are incorrect in this line of thinking, however. In recent years, a new parsing of Seligman's initial findings with more cutting-edge testing methods overturned his initial conclusion that people learn to become helpless when repeatedly shocked. His theory is now known as "learned mastery;" it was the dogs who escaped after being shocked who had learned a new, more adaptive habit. They were the ones who responded to adversity by jumping out of the cages, not lying down, which had made them "masterful" in their environments, not helpless. Now the belief is that helplessness is our default setting at birth, not something we develop as the result of setbacks. We must learn mastery by persisting through obstacles, which is how we learn to thrive and succeed – and you can't buy, fake, or wait for someone to do this for you.

Plenty of accepted research backs this up. Ed Deci and Richard Ryan's Self-Determination Theory, another widely proven finding, says that all humans have three basic needs they must satisfy. They are autonomy (the ability to control one's environment), relatedness (caring and being connected to others), and competence (experiencing mastery in personal goals). Thus, if learning how to achieve important goals to feel masterful satisfies a basic human need, and we are born helpless, it means that one of the greatest tools we can learn or teach others to thrive is the science of how to accomplish the big goals. This is my mission.

> Deci and Ryan note that "autonomous motivation" is optimal for goal pursuit. This occurs when you are aware and engaged in what you are pursuing, and how you are taking action. This leads to greater persistence, more flexibility and creativity, greater well-being, better health, and long-term positive effects across culture, lifespan, and gender.

We Have Entered a Global Learning Goal Condition

There are also current crises in the world that support the urgency of learning how to do hard things. As the coronavirus pandemic raged across the world beginning in 2020, no one remained untouched by the sudden impact of countries closing their borders, workers being ordered to stay home, and schools changing how they instructed students of all ages. Cities emptied. Hospitals filled. Organizations that once thought onboarding new employees could only be done in person welcomed new hires in mass Zoom meetings. Handshake deals turned into e-signatures on documents in the cloud. People who had never bought a dress online suddenly entrusted their family's grocery shopping to masked strangers who left triple-bagged food on their doorsteps. In short, everything we'd once done automatically to achieve an assured outcome didn't work any longer. If you did not adapt and accept that the world would never be the same again, and that you'd have to learn new ways to succeed, you wouldn't survive, let alone thrive.

In GST parlance, we had entered a mass "learning goal" condition that Locke and Latham say is a period in which you must add knowledge and skills before expecting yourself to achieve any specific outcome by a certain date. I quickly grasped the suddenness and significance of this shift from a scientific perspective and explained to clients and friends how to apply GST to their lives to avoid becoming frustrated by holding themselves to unrealistic, old standards. I didn't see that knowledge being shared anywhere else, though.

Quiet Quitting and the 'She-cession'

The pandemic caused a significant drop in productivity in 2020, according to McKinsey, due to business lockdowns, economic uncertainty, and remote work adjustments. As companies developed new ways of working, results were mixed. Some found reduced commute times allowed workers to get more done, but those results were balanced by complaints of distraction, loneliness, burnout, and lack of collaboration. The addition of closed schools and remote education hampered productivity, as well, with women handling the lion's share of disruptions to their careers.

This period quickly became known as a "She-cession" because existing gender inequalities were worsened, highlighting in "bright fluorescent marker the deep-seated disparities between men and women." Some reports equated the drop in women's standings in areas like academic research and publication to the equivalent of 10 years of lost progress, and an April 2024 Bloomberg report said that women's representation in C-Suite roles was experiencing its first drop since 2008, marking an "alarming turning point." Reports of "quiet quitting" by disengaged workers made it hard for companies to find and retain talent, leaving managers shorthanded and overwhelmed. Artificial intelligence advances have also contributed to a roiling business world because not only are management practices still in flux, but now companies also must invest in training and education to take advantage of artificial intelligence's promise of improved efficiency.

McKinsey's 2023 report on Women in the Workplace conducted with LeanIn.org quotes many women who say they are stymied at many turns in the workplace for reasons large and small, including what they describe as a different goal accomplishment metric for promotion for them than for men, whether they are working remotely or in person. "Women are often hired and promoted based on past accomplishments, while men are hired and promoted based on future potential. This bias affects women's career advancement, especially early in their careers."

Role Clarity and Productivity

In early 2024, Gallup's annual "State of the Workplace" report described the workplace in starkly negative terms, noting that employee disengagement was at all-time highs and productivity had continued to plummet. Poor goal setting practices were identified as one of the key drivers of these negative outcomes for several reasons. Gallup said that unclear expectations were holding teams back, reducing satisfaction and weakening employees' commitment to the organization's vision and mission. "Role clarity" was identified as a particularly troubling weak spot because of its importance in engagement.

Even more concerning was that employees who understood what was expected of them at work had dropped dramatically in the previous four years, especially for exclusively remote and hybrid employees. Additionally, the lack of meaningful feedback from managers, especially on goals, priorities, strengths, and collaboration, had contributed to confusion about what was expected of them.

What was Gallup's prescription to address these problems?

This respected research giant recommended starting with an emphasis on learning how to set higher quality goals. The report said that if the goals were set correctly and were reviewed weekly or bi-weekly with managers, there would be more role clarity. Workers would then understand what was expected of them, leading to greater productivity and worker engagement. As I read the report, I added a few of my own hypotheses: well-set goals would result in more accurate performance reviews, which would be especially helpful to women and minorities, who would get the type of feedback that would reflect their contributions and count toward leadership promotions. Using goal setting theory to separate learning goals from performance goals would also contribute to more engagement because of the curiosity and creativity evoked when people are allowed to learn what is expected of them instead of experiencing a demand for immediate results. And everyone would be happier – something research had conclusively found contributed to workplace well-being, group harmony, and enhanced confidence and optimism.

But who was going to give them this information? If most people still don't know GST, which has been my observation since the initial publication of *Creating Your Best Life*, who was going to train them? Certainly not the motivational speakers talking about SMART goals, an approach that had been found to be harmful to people's goal pursuits because of its conflicting terminology in different settings and the inherent inference to set "realistic" or "attainable" goals – not hard goals – or the business leaders who found inspiration from the tiny proportion of people selected for special forces teams.

I decided to try to fill those shoes.

Mark Zuckerberg, CEO of Meta, declared that 2023 would be the "year of efficiency" and Sundar Pichai, CEO of Google, said that productivity was lower than it should be because of bloated management numbers, stressing that reducing head count – not improved goal systems – would solve their productivity challenges. The problem of "BS" and "irrelevant jobs" of the "laptop class" in high tech and industrial corporations has long been a concern of investors, like David Ulevitch of Andreessen Horowitz, who said that "fake jobs" were preventing companies like Meta and Google from passing profits along to pensioners and other shareholders. "So those people aren't just being useless (and being coddled to think useless jobs actually matter – they don't), but they are also taking money away from the rest of the workforce's retirement programs," he said.

History Predicts We Can Succeed

The Bubonic Plague, also known as the "Black Death," was a pandemic that spread through insect-infested rats beginning in the mid-1300s, wiping out between 25% and 60% of the population in Asia and Europe. It spurred sweeping upheavals in cultural, political, artistic, and medical norms. Instead of baseless healing approaches like bloodletting and forced vomiting, medicine evolved in a more evidence-based direction anchored in research and science. Wages grew to reflect the changes in a more powerful worker class, burial practices became more sanitary, industries evolved to incorporate guilds and apprentices, and even art became more realistic in its depiction of people and their lives.

The terrible pestilence and population losses of the Black Death birthed the Renaissance, a period of unparalleled knowledge expansion and human flourishing. We are now in an equivalent period. Our lives have been disrupted and everything from vaccine development to how we deliver higher education is nothing like it was just five years ago. It's now normal for organizations to hire remote workers and create hybrid jobs that only require a day or two a month of onsite work; this approach was once viewed as unique and ineffective, and now it's a benefit touted by companies to lure talent that is unlikely to disappear. Doctors routinely perform surgery and psychotherapy through augmented reality and video conferencing. Buying anything from dog food to prom dresses is rarely done at malls or by interacting with a human any longer, and what we purchase is increasingly brought right to us by drones, self-driving cars, and fleets of Amazon delivery vans in the middle of the night. Money doesn't exchange hands much, either, as we tap credit cards on computerized checkout systems at gas stations and tell Alexa to reorder toilet paper for us. Even writing a check to hand to someone is thought to be an old-fashioned courtesy that will end soon.

If we are honest with ourselves, history is telling us that many of the recent painful and unwanted upheavals in our lives might be leading us to a new Renaissance, and I believe that part of that Renaissance will include rebirthing an approach to goal setting that is more modern, scientific, and effective.

One of the exciting medical advances of recent years has been the birth of "smart bandages," which will soon be able to let doctors remotely monitor wounds, reduce scarring, and accelerate healing through light pulses and dispensing medicine through the touch of a button. "We kind of are [still] practicing medieval medicine in wound care," Dr. Geoffrey Gurtner, chairman of the surgery department at the University of Arizona College of Medicine-Tucson, said about his work with others on smart bandages. The US Department of Defense has invested in the project in the hopes that smart bandages will be used on the battlefield and other hard-to-reach locations before the end of the decade, marking the first major advance in wound care in hundreds of years.

Before COVID-19, I Never Knew I Could . . .

I like to ask clients, "Before COVID-19, I never knew I could. . . ." We all occasionally lose sight of how much more innovative and resourceful we've become since 2020 as familiar tools and rituals have morphed into newer, often improved, ways of doing things. In this abrupt transition, most people reported learning to live with less, focus more on the people who mattered, and improvise how to meet daily needs in new ways.

Just as the Renaissance created a more evidence-based approach to many fields, I believe it's time for us to move into learning and embracing a science-informed approach to goal accomplishment through GST and the BRIDGE (Brainstorming, Relationships, Investments, Decision-Making, Good Grit, and Excellence) framework that I've spent years successfully testing and refining with business professionals, athletes, students, retired adults, and in a variety of cultures. Let's do away with fantasy approaches like "The Law of Attraction" and learn how to master our environments in ways that build curiosity, optimism, and grit. Let's go from dreaming about big goals to undertaking the journey to make them reality, regardless of how hard we must work to overcome challenges and not get a trophy at the end of every day.

I believe that every single one of us is responsible for leading ourselves to our best performances in work and life. We can't expect others to do this for us, so my goal is for every reader to learn the skills and behaviors shared in this book to develop and enjoy the fruits of a more proactive approach to life starting now. This mindset shift will lead you to a more fulfilling and purpose-driven existence and equip you with the tools to overcome procrastination and work disengagement. By the end of this book, you will have learned practical strategies for the steps required to accomplish your big goals, including cultivating better decision-making, knowing which relationships are most likely to support your dreams, and understanding how to avoid "goals gone wild" and "stupid grit." The timeless nature of the principles included here ensure that the book will remain relevant for years to come, and possibly become the beloved new classic in the goal setting field – my own big goal!

How to Use This Book

You'll get the best benefit from this book if you read the chapters in order from beginning to end. Just as bridges in the real world are built on a solid foundation, so is the BRIDGE. I've organized the book in this order:

- ◆ Part I, "The Pillars of Productivity:" These chapters ground you in all of the science and history that forms the foundation for the BRIDGE.
- ◆ Part II, "Crossing the BRIDGE:" Brainstorming, Relationships, Investments, Decision-Making, Good Grit, and Excellence are each explored in their own focused chapter.
- ◆ Part III, "Supplemental Resources:" This part of the book provides many useful resources, beginning with worksheets that support ideas discussed in Part I and moving on to worksheets that help you develop your own BRIDGE as discussed throughout Part II.

Ready to go? Let's get started!

BiG GOALS

PART I

The Pillars of Productivity

Setting and achieving goals is one of the most important skills anyone can possess, which is why the topic has generated thousands of years of speculation about the best ways to do it to be happy, successful, and contribute to society. And because humans alone possess the unique gift of prospection – imagining the future – having the knowledge and tools to make those dreams come true is a superpower everyone wants.

This is exactly why the field of goal setting is such an evergreen topic that generates billions of dollars being spent annually on productivity systems, self-help books, planning calendars, and strategy retreats that are designed to make people get things done. The problem is that even though everyone talks about goals and has an opinion about how to achieve them, very few people or organizations know or use the actual science behind goal accomplishment. And at a time when most industries and professions are being disrupted because of scientific, technological, and cultural upheavals, goal setting remains one of the only dinosaurs that hasn't changed in a meaningful way since the advent of the steam engine.

This book aims to bring significant change to the world by challenging accepted goal setting approaches that have hardened into inaccurate belief systems. The knowledge here will democratize your chances of success because the tools required to set, pursue, and achieve your goals are not stuck in academia where you can't find them, and instead of going to lots of sources to gather what is most important, I've done that for you here.

Our exploration begins in Chapter 1 with a look at the current state of goal setting. Despite the prevalence of goal setting advice, much of it lacks scientific backing. Phrases like "visualize your success" or "write down your goals" sound promising but often fall short without a deeper understanding of what really works. The first chapter will dismantle common myths and set the stage for a more informed approach. By examining the limitations of popular methods, you'll see why a shift toward evidence-based practices is essential for achieving meaningful and sustainable success.

In Chapter 2, we look at the early twentieth century roots of effective goal setting with Frederick Winslow Taylor's "scientific management," or Taylorism. Although Taylor's methods emphasized efficiency and productivity, they often overlooked the human element. This chapter traces the evolution from Taylorism to more holistic approaches, including the pioneering work of Mary Parker Follett and Lillian Moller Gilbreth, who emphasized the importance of human factors in management. By understanding this historical context, you'll appreciate the need for a balanced approach that values both efficiency and well-being.

Unlocking the "secret" to successful goal setting involves delving into Goal Setting Theory (GST) developed by Edwin Locke and Gary Latham, which we'll explore in Chapter 3. This theory, grounded in decades of research, highlights the importance of setting specific, challenging goals and the role of feedback in goal achievement. We'll explore the core principles of GST, including the distinction between learning goals and performance goals, and why these concepts are crucial for driving motivation and high performance.

In Chapter 4, I will build on the principles of GST by explaining the factors that led me to create my BRIDGE framework, which turbocharges goal accomplishment and fills in the gaping holes around how to accomplish a goal once it's been set. I also share how I became aware that our long-accepted goal systems that don't acknowledge gender and cultural differences are as off-kilter as are the artificial intelligence tools that spit out inaccurate images and facts because they haven't been trained to serve a population that is as varied and nuanced as our goals are. It is time for us to pull together the awareness and knowledge that give us the best possible chance of success, and to do so, we need to identify the best from the old and merge it with newer and better tools that work.

As you move forward, keep these foundational concepts in mind. They are the pillars upon which the rest of the book is built. By integrating these insights, you'll be better prepared to harness the power of goal setting to achieve your aspirations, no matter how ambitious they may be. Whether you're aiming to excel in your career, improve your personal life, or embark on a new venture, the evidence-based strategies and practical tools in this book will guide you on your journey to success.

CHAPTER 1

The State of Goal Setting Today

How Do You Get There from Here?

What do you say to yourself when you decide to go after a big goal? Or someone else tells you that they are taking a leap to accomplish a long-held dream?

Chances are, the comments are like the well-meaning responses below:

- Go for it.
- Suck it up.
- Have more willpower.
- Bite down on the mouthpiece.
- Make a vision board.
- Where there's a will, there's a way.
- One day at a time.
- Imagine it and you'll attract it to you.
- Write down your goals because that makes them happen.
- Repeat positive affirmations.
- Be accountable to someone else.

While most of these phrases have a nugget of helpful truth in them, it's not enough to throw out an inspiring slogan in the hopes it will enhance your motivation, nor will it inspire anyone else to do their best. We also cannot assume that the steps that worked for us when we overcame obstacles will always lead others to accomplish their own big goals. Yet advice pours in from everywhere when you are ready to make a change, particularly at New Year's resolution time, which is usually associated with losing weight, starting an exercise program, or quitting a bad habit.

My head spins some days from the ceaseless stream of ads for products that promise to help you get where you want to go. Before and after weight loss pictures populate my television and computer screens with promises that a new supplement, fitness program, or psychological approach will cure me and improve my life. Online articles, blog posts, and podcast interviews with "experts" in goal setting vie for my hopeful clicks. Celebrities smile from the covers of magazines sharing stories of their transformations so we will all admire their resilience and look to them for guidance. Bookstores advertise their latest crop of visualization guides and planning journals as better than the ones they offered the previous year. It all makes cash registers ring because self-help continues to be one of the most evergreen topics people are willing to invest in, and currently the reinvention business for those at midlife and beyond is lucrative and growing.

How does anyone really know who to trust or what to do?

> Setting a goal has a big impact on conscious and subconscious behavior. It creates focus, it causes us to scan our minds for what skills and people we will need to know, it creates hope and screens out "spam" that doesn't match the goal, and we are energized with zest and curiosity.

THE PERILS OF PUBLISH OR PERISH

It makes sense that esteemed academics like Angela Duckworth, Adam Grant, Carol Dweck, and Jonathan Haidt, who have all published books on topics like happiness and character strengths, would be trustworthy when it comes to learning about how to achieve success. Their topics are all relevant to goal accomplishment, so inevitably one of their books breaks through and becomes a runaway hit, like Angela Duckworth's *Grit* (2016), which became "must" reading in schools and organizations and led her TED talk to become one of the most popular of all time. Graduate school professors from prominent universities like Dartmouth, Stanford, and the University of Michigan have also made their voices heard in the media and at corporate gatherings on goal-related subjects like psychological safety and the secrets of high-performing teams.

There's a little-discussed problem with making these types of sources your only source of information and guidance on goal accomplishment, however. Academic researchers are incentivized to focus on their own unique contributions to their fields and must "publish or perish" to attain lifetime tenure and job security. It makes sense that they would hyper-focus on their own niche because their prominence often yields research grants and labs full of graduate students helping them to continue to study what interests them. The public responds by buying these academics' books to learn about things like confidence, "imposter syndrome," and intrinsic motivation, but since each one only covers a sliver of the knowledge required to achieve big goals, our bookshelves will fill up, our pockets will empty, and we will only have one or two pieces of the puzzle, even though they are all excellent resources by themselves!

BLINDERS IN THE IVORY TOWER

One day I made of point of listening to a series of well-regarded podcasts featuring all the top researchers on resilience, a topic that matters to anyone who wants to know how to be mentally and physically tough. At least one-third of the interviews were devoted to these men and women being queried on how their work was distinct from, and similar to, other academics' findings on the same subject. Instead of being tactful, I frequently heard passive-aggressive comments about the other researchers, defensiveness about what they believed was the right way to discuss the topic, or an outright refusal to acknowledge that anyone else's findings were worth mentioning in the same breath.

The more I listened, the more obvious it became that establishing yourself as an authority on a certain subject probably means for some that you must wear blinders about the importance and nuances of other people's work, regardless of how good it is. This attitude pays off in the Darwinian academic environment, but the real losers are people like you and me who want to find evidence-based ways to thrive, and who would benefit from having the top findings on a topic synthesized without bias so that we can discern the best lessons for ourselves. Without this type of thoughtful solution, though, people like me spend valuable time and money attending conferences, taking online courses, and reading reams of research to extract the insights that can make a difference in our own lives. Given the fast-moving findings in social psychology and other fields that touch on goal setting, though, stitching everything together to create a workable success plan based on research feels like Sisyphus rolling his rock uphill, only to have it roll back down immediately and leave us with another hill to climb.

Another problem with relying on academics as your sole authority on how to accomplish your own goals is that they don't always test their findings on average men and women to see if the results of their experiments can make a difference when applied in the real world – say, in high-stakes business settings, in the schools of underprivileged youth, or in competitive sports. Too much of their work focuses on the responses of university undergraduates, who often participate in their professors' research as part of taking their classes. While much can be learned from young adults, it's not always easy to extrapolate the meaning of a 20-something's cortisol levels after writing about upsetting situations to how a person raised in a foreign culture would respond in the same condition.

WHAT ELSE IS OUT THERE?
I have spent years taking the temperature of the goal setting world and asking clients and friends where they've gotten their best knowledge about how to achieve success in their lives or their companies. Overwhelmingly they say someone recommended a book by a popular motivational figure (Tony Robbins or Harvey Mackay, for example), or they heard a speaker at a business forum (usually peddling a self-published book or their own system). People also say blog posts and online articles about New Year's resolutions give them ideas, as do the stories of the successful entrepreneurs on *Shark Tank*. Regardless of where they get their information, I always ask

if they have heard of Locke and Latham's goal setting theory. The answer is always no.

"THE HARVARD STUDY OF 1950"

One of my clients is the co-CEO of a financial advisory firm who loves to learn about any topic pertaining to maximizing productivity. He is in a group of business leaders known as YPO (Young Presidents Organization) and has enrolled in several certificate programs promoted by his peers. He always comes back enthusiastic and energized from these seminars, usually toting a new leather-bound goal setting binder or a color-coded organizational system.

At the start of one of our early coaching sessions he mentioned that he'd learned some exciting science about goal setting the previous weekend and that he was going to create new writing habits because of it.

"The speaker quoted research from the University of Virginia that proved that writing down your goals and telling others about those goals was the number-one scientific approach to accomplishing hard things," he reported. "He said only 3% of people do this, but when they do, they are likely to achieve everything they write down!"

I know that there are many approaches that can be effective, and I don't like to burst someone's bubble if something is working for them, but this client – like so many others – had been sold a $10,000 program I was sure was not based on rigorous evidence. One of the urban legends I'd tracked down after learning about Locke and Latham's goal setting theory was this very chestnut about writing down your goals and telling people, which was occasionally known as "The Harvard Study of 1950," and referenced as "proof" in many of the books I'd once thought were factual.

"Can you give me the name of the presenter and the information he shared on that research?" I asked.

Although skeptical, I was willing to be proven wrong. I called the presenter with the fancy system to introduce myself, explain my background, and ask if he could share his research with me.

He never returned my call, and it's undoubtedly because the "research" he had boasted about didn't exist. But lots of people running businesses and setting goals for their employees had bought his spiel and did believe it, so the damage was already done.

"[U]nifying a company behind one project management tool is proving to be difficult, according to CEOs who cite Asana, Airtable, monday.com, and Atlassian's Jira products among the more popular tools" currently being used in the workplace, with each one costing a company anywhere from $12 to $45 per user monthly. Most companies use several of these, and annual costs rise quickly once the client commits to any one productivity system. Once workers and teams are trained and that system is embedded in a company's infrastructure, disengaging from the product becomes dramatically more difficult.

#DUDEPODCASTS AND #MANELS

My client is typical of where most people in the business world learn how to set goals. A quick internet search of "goal setting approaches" results in page after page of references to blog posts and instructional videos like "How to Really Make Your Dreams Come True This Year," "The Secrets of Lasting Success," and "What Winners Do Differently." I dip in and out of these links to see what is there, and it's almost always just storytelling of someone's successful endeavor along with a guidebook or product for sale.

Podcasts are a favorite learning tool for many, but I rarely find any episodes on goal setting that include references to research. There are exceptions, of course, like *The Tim Ferriss Show*, which usually has long-form interviews with a variety of credible experts, but the information is delivered and synthesized through the prism of the host: a white, Ivy League–educated man. I'm a big admirer of Ferriss, who became known for the productivity approach he popularized in *The Four-Hour Workweek*, and I have learned a lot from the guests he brings on his show, but I had a Eureka! moment one day while driving six hours to and from our beach house in Delaware, listening to his show and others like it the whole time.

I often speak into my Apple Watch to capture ideas I want to follow up on, but when I scanned the transcript of my voice notes from that trip, I saw a huge problem I'd never noticed before. Those hours of thinking, listening intently, and dictating memos hadn't included a single reference to a woman. I hadn't heard one woman expert interviewed, nor had I heard stories about any woman's boldness, intrepidity, or scientific contribution to the world. I'd heard story after story about courageous special forces warriors, US presidents who had overcome great odds to lead societal change, turnaround CEOs, and historical figures of note, but every single one of them had been exclusively about men – and, overwhelmingly, white men. Not only that, but these stories had also been told by men to other men!

I started to call shows like these "dudepodcasts," modeled after movements started by women who had coined hashtags like #manpanel (or #manel) and #dudewall to bring attention to the lack of women's presence on stage at prestigious gatherings, or in pictures on walls devoted to outstanding leadership. Like many other women, I'd simply become inured to the fact that if I wanted to read about how to become successful, or listen to a podcast about overcoming challenges, my teachers and their content would most likely be about people who didn't look like me, sound like me, or tell stories that I could identify with. I don't want to discount the importance of the information related during these shows, but once you begin to look hard at the science of goal setting and motivation, the differences I spotted couldn't be more important.

"WOMEN IN RED" AND GENIUSES

That day of looking through my voice note transcripts marked a turning point for me in terms of what I recognized as the unintentional impact that this "priming" was having on me. Priming research shows that we are consciously and unconsciously shaped to behave and think in specific ways because of prompts in our environments. These can include aromas, colors, sounds, and people. Marketers take advantage of priming research to get consumers to associate certain products with something we want or need – being thirsty with drinking a Coca-Cola, for example. The results of priming can be insidious and unintended; little girls who are asked to draw a picture of a "leader" rarely draw a picture of a woman because that is not what they usually see celebrated in books, television shows, or internet games.

Gary Latham has done a lot of research to establish that goal priming is an important part of achieving goals. In a surprising turn, he didn't just find that priming for achievement – for example, placing a picture of a victorious runner crossing a finish line on the cover of fundraising guidelines – greatly improved results, he found that having a subconscious goal could also be positively impacted by primes at the same time.

I wanted to look more deeply into my suspicion that the most popular podcasts on achieving success were dominated by men talking to and about men, so I hired a doctoral student to research the top 10 business and self-help podcasts and report back on the ratio of male to female hosts and guests. After a few days of scrolling through page after page of shows and taking meticulous notes, she sent me the eye-popping numbers: most podcasts had a ratio of three or four men to one woman, but the number-one podcast in the world featured an average of more than five men to one woman!

"Create Create Create"?

Learning that my felt experience of being "unseen" matched the absurdly low ratios of female-to-male voices everywhere I turned made me think more deeply about the impact this discrepancy might be having on podcast listeners – half of whom are women, according to the latest statistics. I also wondered what minority women – the least likely to be guests – internalized as they took in this type of information during dog walks, cooking meals, and work commutes. Were they and other underrepresented groups unconsciously setting smaller goals than they might otherwise because of how the knowledge was delivered? Did it impact their confidence in what they thought they could tackle? Were their goals big enough?

The persistent gender stereotype that women are not as competent as men in the high-paying fields of science, technology, and engineering has an impact on whether a woman in those professions will have the confidence to share her ideas in group discussions or accept praise without discounting it. These stereotypes persist in obvious and stealthy ways, including the 1991 Teen Talk Barbie doll that was programmed to blurt, "Math class is tough! Do you have a crush on anyone?" and when Harvard president Larry Summers said in a 2005 speech that women were wired to have less math aptitude than men. This "occupational sorting" of putting oneself in certain professions lowers women's confidence about their ability to achieve their goals in a stereotypically men's field, a problem that also impacts men who enter fields dominated by women, like teaching and social work.

My concerns about these types of gender discrepancies and their impact on our goal setting practices crystallized one afternoon after listening to a top psychology podcast on the topic of "genius." The host, a friend whose work I admire, was interviewing the acknowledged world expert on the subject, who confidently explained his data-driven algorithm for being identified as a genius. His criteria ruled out anyone who had not spent decades pursuing their craft so that they could "create create create" and amass a prodigious output. He also cited the need for a prospective genius to have their biographies in encyclopedias, and for their "brilliant breakthroughs" to be cited by other luminaries of the time.

I fumed. How could this man's mathematical model possibly be an accurate predictor of "genius" when women and people of color have historically lacked the money and societal support to be educated and apprenticed, or had the good fortune to invest time in their craft to "create, create, create" while a spouse or partner had their back? And being referenced in encyclopedias was a criterion to be a genius? Women's Wikipedia biographies are so sparse in comparison to men's (80%+biographies are of men) that Wikipedia has launched the "Women in Red" project to encourage the public to contribute stories to transform red names of notable women into blue hyper-linked biographies. (Donna Strickland, the 2018 recipient of the Nobel Prize in Physics for her work on generating laser beams with ultrashort pulses, had her biography rejected by Wikipedia earlier that year because she did not meet their standards for "notability.")

It particularly irked me to hear that academic citations – or cita-tions of any kind – were considered a barometer of genius. Research on the topic of academic publishing has consistently shown that the contributions of women are frequently overlooked and underval-ued in research journals. In fact, a 2022 study in *Nature* noted that because women were routinely overlooked when giving credit, they received fewer promotions, lower compensation, and less recogni-tion than men, a situation that almost certainly must have under-mined what they believed they could accomplish and also receive credit for.

VICARIOUS LEARNING

Although I was already committed to absorbing and sharing the fin-est available science on goal setting with clients and audiences, my sudden wake-up call about just how ubiquitous and pervasive these often-unhelpful primes are for many people's goal setting was one more nudge to write this book. After all, when you don't see or hear inspiring stories and voices of people who are relatable, it's harder to believe you can accomplish that same goal. Self-efficacy – the cer-tainty that you can find a way to do something, even if you haven't previously done it – is partly built through "vicarious learning." This is why groups like Alcoholics Anonymous work for so many; if you are seeking a role model of sobriety to give you hope, you'll prob-ably meet someone who looks and sounds like you within your first week of attending meetings.

At this point you must be wondering how you'll ever achieve your own big goals if academic research is spread across numerous silos, the methods you've heard about like SMART goals aren't real science, and the world is tilted toward a one-dimensional view of the kinds of people you can learn from and emulate to create your best life.

My solution came during one of the lowest moments of my adult life, leading directly to the BRIDGE methodology in this book.

There are many accepted challenges to the use of SMART as an acronym for goal setting. One of them is that SMART stands for different words in many different contexts; the R is used as "realistic," "reachable," and "relevant" in some settings, the A is "actionable," "attainable," "assignable," or "appropriate," and M can be "meaningful" or "measurable." And when a person sets "attainable" or "realistic" goals for themselves, they will rarely set challenging goals, particularly if a bonus or monetary reward will be impacted. Thus, SMART goals can encourage "low" goals without enough guidance to even determine if the goal is a good idea to begin with!

THE HUBERMAN LAB CRAZE

In 2021, I was hospitalized for a mysterious virus that sapped my energy and scrambled my immune system. After three days, an infectious disease doctor ran one last test on a blood sample and discovered that I had cytomegalovirus, something that is common in children but that can lead to grave challenges in adults. There is no cure except rest, so I hit the pause button on my life and made sure that getting my health back was my top priority.

I practiced a Dutch concept called *uitwaaien* – airing out your soul in windy, salty, cold air – for months while I took bracing walks on the shores of the Atlantic Ocean. A paragon of physical health ever since I'd overcome bulimia 40 years earlier, I was shaken by my close call with lasting damage to my body and immune system. My mission became updating my knowledge and coming up with new ways to be stress-hardy and happy.

As I walked along the Atlantic Ocean, I discovered *The Huberman Lab* podcast by Dr. Andrew Huberman, a professor at Stanford Medical School. The show frequently ran for multiple hours at a time, but I was hooked. And it turns out scores of other people were, too. Within a year of launching, Huberman had amassed millions of followers. His thoughtful approach to topics ranging from improving gut health to the benefits of cold plunges included practical explanations of the best and latest research. He also took time to note any contradictions and how to separate fact from the fiction we often hear in the media about popular health practices. Fans like me loved the "protocols" we could immediately experiment with to get our own results. The more I listened and tried evidence-based behavior changes like getting early natural light exposure to reset my sleep clock, the better I felt and the more I experienced "learned mastery" over my health.

THE BRIDGE BETWEEN ACADEMIA AND US

Huberman understood that people are hungry for facts that will help them live healthier, better lives, and he solved the problem that still plagues the goal setting world: he brought cutting-edge research out of academia and from behind paywalls and distilled it so that everyone without that access could benefit. I took my cue from his impactful approach. My mission now is to have a similar impact on the world of goal setting so that more people can learn how to succeed and thrive based on the best research from motivation to willpower to grit, and to do it in a more heterogenous way that blends all the findings together in a bias-free way.

Although I do not have a PhD, I do have a degree that is designed to accomplish what I've set out to do in this book. My master's degree from the University of Pennsylvania is in Applied Positive Psychology, which means I "apply" the research from the fields of success and thriving to help people improve their lives. That is why this book is your bridge from the Ivory Tower to Main Street, so sit back and take the next few hours to acquaint yourself with what you need to know to experience success. Experiment as you read along, create your own protocols, and take careful note of what works best for you. We all differ in personality, outlook, and circumstance, so learning the keystone basics and personalizing their tenets so they will work for you is the goal.

Before we cross that bridge, though, we need a short history of where we were 100 years ago with goal setting and where that has brought us today. By the end of the next chapter, you won't just have a context for why goals matter, you'll understand how they work at a granular level and you will have more hope that they can and will work for you.

CHAPTER 2

The Emergence of a Better Way

Time, Motion, and "Taylorism"

A young bespectacled man sat quietly observing the employees of the Midvale Steel Company as they went through the motions of their day. It was 1881 and the United States was in a post-war industrial expansion boom that would soon make it the world's leading economy. The man intently watching each employee and noting the time it took them to do every task was Frederick Winslow Taylor, a 24-year-old engineer who was exploring how the application of scientific principles could create a more efficient workplace. His resulting calculations on how to speed up production gave him the moniker "the father of scientific management" and launched the new field of "time-and-motion" studies in the workplace, later known as "Taylorism."

Taylor believed that every worker could be taught to avoid wasted movement and energy in their jobs, and that they ought to be compensated for learning how to increase the output that would lead to more company profits. Although his ideas were influential and led to new mass production techniques, detractors pointed out that by focusing on speed to the exclusion of a worker's humanity, he reduced employees to robots who simply took orders from managers. Unions also pushed back, saying that Taylorism would take advantage of hard-working employees who

17

had no guarantee that increased company profits stemming from greater efficiency would be passed along, and that this emphasis could lead to lower safety standards and disempowered, unhappy employees.

Regardless of the criticisms or doubts voiced about the potential downsides of connecting productivity with income, denying employees autonomy in how they performed their jobs, and failing to invest in better workplace conditions, Taylorism steamrolled its critics and had widespread adoption, something from which we are still picking up the pieces.

Doing Good versus *Doing Well*

The push-pull between companies' desire for optimal productivity versus concern for the worker has been a hotly debated topic since Taylor's "time-and-motion" studies spread across the world. Although many well-meaning leaders and workplace philosophies have since tried to marry the drive for bottom-line profits with qualitative variables like worker well-being or democratic decision-making, there is still no agreement today about how to balance these two objectives.

As a result, the same goal setting practices and emphasis on bottom-line results to gauge productivity have repeated themselves from one generation to the next with only minor changes, such as giving workers the option of flexible work times or offering paid maternal leave. Innumerable entrepreneurs have jumped in to try to solve this pain point with CRM (customer relationship management) tools, fancy goal setting dashboards, and webinars on positive workplaces that cost organizations tens of thousands of dollars annually. Books by researchers and consultants about companies that "do good" and "do well" have also become a cottage industry, contributing to some nations deciding to measure their Gross Happiness Product along with their Gross National Product. But none of the changes have conclusively moved the needle around creating a harmonious approach to goal setting that would satisfy both ends of the spectrum.

A May 2024 *Wall Street Journal* article noted that end user annual corporate spending on goal setting and productivity software systems came to $4.6 billion, creating problems for CTOs and CIOs who were trying to rein in spending costs. "It's an eternal problem," said Mansoor Basha, chief technology officer of software marketing company Stagwell Marketing Cloud. "If you go to any organization, you will find at least five or six different project management tools being used at the same time," with subscription costs rocketing annually, depending on the number of users. Jeff Sippel, CIO of Northwestern Mutual, added that part of the problem the company was facing was the variability and different strengths or weaknesses of the tools, leading to different teams advocating for their favorite one; as a result, Northwestern Mutual currently underwrites up to three project management tools every year.

Dominating or Cooperating?

Irrespective of how managers have operated since 1900, there has been one theme that has never changed: one gender has always controlled the conversations and methods around the best ways to achieve productivity. Given the historic power differentials that have always favored men, and the fact that they prefer and perform better on goals related to achievement, competition, power, status, and money, it's understandable that their opinions would have held sway for so long. This dynamic has often played out in politics, sports, and business where men have sought to outperform others by emphasizing winning and domination. Their best efforts have also primarily revolved around seeking quantifiable extrinsic rewards like money and promotion.

Women, on the other hand, are known to favor goals that are more intrinsic and "soft," like being happy, finding meaning, and experiencing emotional growth. This has contributed to their pursuit of careers like teaching, nursing, and social work. It's also true that women tend to shun competition and risk-taking, performing better on goals related to cooperation and communal harmony. Some of these differences can be chalked up to what cultures have typically identified as "feminine" or "masculine" behaviors, and sociologists also point to the modest role played by biology.

A Disrupted World Requires a Disruption in Goal Setting Practices

In this complex and fast-moving twenty-first century world, where power is increasingly fluid, women make up half the workforce in most countries, and research has become more nuanced around optimal ways to achieve success, this male-dominated thinking around how to set goals and strive for achievement is woefully ineffective. Similar to the disruption being experienced in banking, education, marketing, and manufacturing, the time has come to take a hard look at whether the advice that we've been given makes sense, or if a more holistic and evidence-based strategy is better.

To understand what it will take to do this, and why the fight is worth it, we need to take a quick tour of what got us here, and where we missed the boat.

Boys, Business, and Bull's-Eyes

Beginning with Taylorism, productivity approaches have the same blueprint: select a big goal or bull's-eye to go after, and then identify and pursue the sub-goals to get there as quickly as possible. For example, Henry T. Ford streamlined the layout of the factory floor at the Ford Motor Company and stripped the creation of cars down to making component parts and assembling them as quickly as possible. He believed that simply telling workers what was expected of them in a well-designed factory was superior to other ways of thinking. This became known as "Fordism."

Agency Through Acronyms

Starting in the 1950s and continuing to this day, uninspiring acronyms like MBOs (Management by Objectives), OKRs (Objectives and Key Results), and KPIs (Key Performance Indicators) have become the accepted language of goal setting. We are all expected to know it and use it. I frequently hear radio commercials advertising free downloads about how to use a company's products if we want to achieve our own personal KPIs. No one even bothers to explain the acronym because the assumption is that we all know what it means and why it works!

A management consultant named George Doran popularized the acronym SMART in 1981, but the wide variance in what the letters of the acronym represent has created confusion and a lack of agreement in how it is used. Huggy Rao and Robert Sutton, Stanford University professors, call this conundrum "jargon mishmash syndrome" (when a term means different things to different people, resulting in confusion). Most varieties of SMART omit any word that supports Locke and Latham's finding about best outcomes coming from "challenging," not "attainable" goals. As a result, some have likened using SMART as a goal approach as being akin to using spell-check on a document. It can get you started, but it is no guarantee of content or excellence!

#dudegoals and #dudeadvice

When I realized for the first time that every widely accepted approach to goal setting had been designed and promoted by men since the advent of the steam engine, I felt the same surprise and clarity as the day I realized that all the highest-rated podcasts on entrepreneurship, productivity, and business success were #dudepodcasts. Why had I – and everyone else – had such a glaring blind spot about this? Were we too numb to see how this might be a problem? Or did we just not know what to do about it?

Do Mars and Venus Succeed Differently?

It didn't take long for me to sort through the conclusions of sociologists, psychologists, and biologists to confirm that men and women approach goals in very different ways and women would need a different framework if they wanted to succeed at anything. It's undeniable that women and men are socialized, rewarded, and wired differently around agentic behavior, which refers to the ways in which we exert control over our environments, act on our own behalf, and influence others. When we are agentic, we usually have positive outcomes by acting assertively and taking initiative, which leads to more power, status, and career advancement. Men are usually the ones who are allowed to behave this way. Women who are too goal-directed and ambitious don't get the same positive outcomes men do because of "role congruity," and they experience stiff social penalties from both men and women when they violate social norms.

The differences don't stop with the types of goals men and women pursue. How they respond to all kinds of situations that impact how they create a plan and take the steps to overcome challenges is also at wide variance. Recent research has also found that women "tend and befriend" in stressful situations while men "fight and flee." Men benefit from transactional relationships to build success networks, while women fail miserably when they mimic this approach – especially with high-ranking individuals – and do not invest time in getting to know people. Men who aggressively lean into negotiations to get more of what they want are seen as bold and successful; women must negotiate on behalf of others to avoid being penalized for the same behavior. Men who "give" without strings in the workplace are rewarded and viewed favorably, but women who have boundaries around how often they help others are unlikable. (And when they do give, they never get the same positive boost that men do!)

Finally, women must walk an impossible tightrope of being warm, authoritative, and competent to be seen as leaders or promoted to positions of power, while men routinely are ushered into positions of power because of the "confirmation bias" that keeps men rewarding men because they are "like me." Research also shows that when women do become CEOs, they end up on the "glass cliff" – leading organizations that are in such bad shape that they are destined to fail, and if they have the misfortune to become CEOs after a "failed" female CEO, the "halo effect" immediately predisposes people to judge their leadership harshly, something that never impacts male CEOs who follow the disappointing results of another man.

In a study of more than 200 publicly traded companies on the major stock exchanges in the United States and Europe, results showed that when women are on boards of directors several positive outcomes occur. Women come to meetings better prepared and more knowledgeable, leading them to ask more insightful questions that shape results. Women are unafraid of "rocking the boat" by acknowledging they need more information before making decisions, and their presence reduces competitiveness among the men and creates a more open atmosphere with accountability and curiosity, leading to better corporate governance and improved decision-making.

One Stanford university sociology professor, Cecelia Ridgeway, noted in *Framed by Gender* that because of women's lack of workplace power and an embedded system that resists giving it to them, all practices from goal setting strategies to pay practices are unequal and inadequate. Her view of the current system is chilling: "One of the more powerful effects . . . is to infuse gendered meanings into new workplace practices, structure, and rules as these are developed . . . [O]nce such gendered institutional procedures develop, they act to re-create gender inequality in workplace outcomes independently of the personal biases of individual [workers]."

How WEIRD Are Your Goals?

In the last 20 years, increasing attention has been paid to the ways in which a person's culture impacts their views on success and happiness. Similar to the ways in which goal approaches have traditionally favored a white male perspective, Positive Psychology's measures of happiness and life satisfaction have favored the outlook and norms of WEIRD – Western, Educated, Industrialized, Rich, and Democratic – cultures. Recent meta-analyses have shown that while WEIRD cultures promote and reward success when a person achieves hard, valued goals, other cultures don't, which has major implications in personal and work settings where goal setting is expected.

Yukiko Uchida, Masataka Nakayama, and Kimberly S. Bowen explained in a 2024 article in *Current Directions in Psychological Science* that the "characteristics of interdependent happiness emerge because an individual's state of happiness is considered to be inseparable from, and interdependent with, the happiness of other people in the context to which the individual belongs. Hence, there is an understanding that sustainable happiness is achieved by seeking harmony with other individuals who share the same context." They continue, "[I]n many Western societies, people say that happiness allows them to contribute to society, gives them confidence, and empowers them to change the world. In a Japanese context, people avoid maximizing because it does not feel like a verification of self-worth, and if they seek more and more there could be negative impacts toward other people." These and similar findings show that as we expand the vision of appropriate and valued goal setting by necessity, it's not only gender that must be considered as a key variable, it's also the culture in which a person or organization is located that matters.

A Rising Tide Will Lift All Goal Setting Boats

The good news about these expanded findings is that when cultural diversity and a more balanced gender approach exists in corporations, science, medicine, law, teaching, and elsewhere, the end results are always better for everyone. Boardrooms make better decisions, companies make more money, fewer patients die in surgery, countries survive pandemics in better shape, and legal remedies are fairer and less punitive. This bodes well for any efforts to address inconsistencies and the unconscious bias that has shaped and continues to shape how we set, pursue, and achieve goals. We are clearly ready for a massive disruption.

Timing Is Everything

Two brave, brilliant women saw that failing to honor the needs and concerns of both genders would eventually result in unhappiness, poor quality control, and corruption, but they were 100 years before their time. These contemporaries of Taylor were vocal in their call to democratize and humanize the workplace, and to diversify rigid and unfair goal setting practices, but they have been mostly forgotten.

Let's look at Lillian Moller Gilbreth and Mary Parker Follett, who are seen by many as the pioneers whose work and thinking laid the groundwork for Positive Psychology, human relations, group behavior, and workplace wellness movements by advocating for the inclusion of human relationship management with scientific management. They saw all too clearly the dangers of a workplace that only valued time, motion, and efficiency at the expense of human beings, but they didn't have the power, platforms, or financial backing to overcome Taylorism's rigid approach. What can we learn from them now?

Girls, Groups, and Goodwill

Mary Parker Follett and Lillian Moller were born on opposite sides of the country to wealthy families that enrolled them in the finest schools of their time. Moller was so bright that she skipped grades and entered the University of California at Berkeley as a 16-year-old, earning her degree in 1900 and becoming the first woman to speak at a University of California commencement. Follett attended a variety of female academies in Massachusetts while caring for her younger siblings after her father passed away. She later graduated from Radcliffe College, *summa cum laude* with an emphasis on government, economics, law, and philosophy.

Transformational Leadership and Win–Win

Follett became known as the "Mother of Modern Management" and was a trailblazer in the fields of organizational theory and organizational behavior, which she combined with her social work training (she introduced the idea of "community centers"), political activism, and philosophical studies. Follett is credited with the innovative idea that a company's goals are not fixed or pre-determined, but that they emerge from the synergy between people in groups. She called this concept "circular response" and explained that every person's authority, identity, and influence were impacted by others' actions and reactions, creating a dynamic feedback loop of "coactive power." She summarized, "The study of human relations in business and the study of the technology of operating are bound up together."

Unlike Taylorism, Follett preached that people – not efficient systems – are the most valuable commodities in any workplace, and that the greatest contribution a person could make to society was through their work, regardless of their position in a company. To make this possible, she encouraged organizations to invest in promoting positive relationships to improve productivity.

Because Follett wasn't formally trained, didn't have a business background, and her interests spanned multiple areas, her ideas were mostly shared through private talks and writings, which were rediscovered and published in the late 1990s. She is only now receiving belated credit for the concept of "transformational leadership," which she said in 1927 was the result of "followership," "leadership," and collective goals. She also came up with the phrase "win-win" to describe using conflict as a tool to come to mutually beneficial outcomes, and her work is seen as the forerunner of today's "systems theory," which posits that complex results emerge from individual interactions for common good.

> "Many people tell me what I ought to do and just how I ought to do it, but few have made me want to do something."
>
> *Mary Parker Follett*

It's almost comical to note that Follett was also an early victim of "mansplaining." Chester Barnard, an advisor to President Franklin D. Roosevelt, published an influential business book, *The Functions of the Executive*, without disclosing that his call for emphasizing the "soft" skills of communication and informal processes in organizations was cribbed straight from Follett's writings. To his credit, though, the late Warren Bennis, known as "the father of twentieth century leadership studies" and advisor to four US Presidents, attempted to set the record straight on the puzzling omission of Follett's pioneering ideas from the history of productivity, employee well-being, and transformational leadership. He said, "Just about everything written today about leadership and organizations comes from Mary Parker Follett's writing and lectures."

America's First Lady of Engineering

Moller was the first person – man or woman – to earn a doctorate in the field of industrial management, which she later combined with psychology to create the influential field of industrial and organizational psychology. After marrying and taking her husband's last name of Gilbreth, she published her dissertation, "The Psychology of Management: The Function of the Mind in Determining, Teaching and Installing Methods of Least Waste" in 1911, which was the first publication to argue that Taylorism's approach to ignoring the "human element" in management was counterproductive to workplace flourishing and success.

A mother of twelve who was widowed early, Gilbreth combined her roles as parent, researcher, and efficiency expert to create systems that simplified domestic tasks so that more women could be freed up to seek paid work. Not only is she credited with the foot pedal on trash cans and waist-high light switches, but her innovative kitchen "work triangle" that juxtaposed zones for cooking, cleaning, and preparation is still used in most kitchen designs.

Follett and Gilbreth joined forces to fight against one of the worst by-products of the factory system: frequent abuse of unskilled workers, including children, who were exploited with low wages, unsafe conditions, and long hours. Their efforts to draw attention to creating more humane working conditions gave rise to the "human relations movement," which sought to portray workers as more complex and dynamic than Taylor and Ford's depictions of workers as cogs in a factory machine.

> "The workers must understand that they add to the perfectness of the entire establishment. Scientific management is built on the recognition of the individual, with all the idiosyncrasies that distinguish a person."
>
> *Lillian Moller Gilbreth*

For decades after her husband's death, Gilbreth continued to work with major organizations to install "The Gilbreth System," which improved workplace efficiency by combining psychology with science to teach managers how to reduce worker fatigue and achieve better results. Gilbreth received far more acclaim than Follett during her lifetime and was celebrated internationally and in American universities where she taught until she passed in her early 90s.

It's ironic that for all her pioneering work and renown as a trailblazing industrial engineer, psychologist, and research scientist, Gilbreth might be best known today as the mother depicted in the popular children's book and movie, *Cheaper by the Dozen*, which illustrates the zany efficiency experiments in the Gilbreth home. Her children fondly noted that for all the trailblazing efficiency work their mother accomplished, their house was an inefficient disaster!

> One 2016 study of the lasting impact these two women had at a time when women's thinking was not always recognized in the business world is that many of the popular and "cutting-edge" leadership approaches of the twentieth and twenty-first century are now seen as outgrowths of their farsighted and humane thinking on productivity and well-being in the workplace.

Greed Is Good?

The 1987 movie *Wall Street* is remembered for the impromptu speech given by the character played by Michael Douglas, a self-important investment banker who proclaimed at a public shareholder's meeting that the corporate excesses and exorbitant pay of the time was something to be proud of.

"Greed is good," he shouted, as he paced back and forth in front of the appreciative audience and a dais of older men. "Greed is right, greed works. Greed clarifies, cuts through, and captures the essence of evolutionary spirit. . . . [G]reed will save the USA."

One analyst assesses this period as the beginning of America's "rotting business culture." Economists look back ruefully at the "go go go" 1980s as a time when politically motivated deregulation, stock manipulation, and accounting changes normalized bad behavior. The

CEO pay increased by 1322% from 1978 to 2020, and companies that had once been seen as the most innovative began to decline.

Bullet Train Thinking

Boeing, long considered one of America's oldest and finest companies, was one of many organizations that took the approach of maximizing shareholder value at the expense of everyone else. They rewarded senior management with lucrative stock options and whopping pay packages. One business analyst wrote that the company "relentlessly disgorged cash to shareholders when it could have spent it on building a better (and safer) product. Investment that could have benefited employees, communities, and other corporate stakeholders were often sacrificed at the altar of efficiency and free cash flow."

General Electric's CEO Jack Welch was the epitome of a self-promotional leader whose actions highlight the damage that was done to another American company once thought of in lofty terms. Disillusioned by the failure of SMART goals to save its floundering divisions, Welch went to Japan in the 1980s to learn about the famed Toyota Productivity System. He returned with "bullet train thinking" and "stretch" goals that created short-term innovation under tremendous time pressure, but often resulted in long-term disasters. Welch sold off the parts of GE that had once made it a leader – research, development, and quality control – and slashed costs. The emphasis on meeting rigid budget numbers meant corners were cut and unreliable products were pushed out the door. Customers lost their trust in the company, GE was fined in 2004 for failing to report the size of Welch's avaricious pay package, and the stock was dropped from the Dow Jones Industrial Average.

> "Broadly speaking, apart from in manufacturing, we are no more productive in business than we were 20 years ago. Even though a tremendous amount of effort has gone into improving employee engagement, based on understanding the employee
>
> *(continued)*

experience, in parallel. Put simply, we think this [current] productivity paradox is being caused by companies not taking the relevant or right actions in response to their workforce insights . . . 2024 is the year where this needs to end [and] HR must become better at helping organizations measure actual productivity through smarter goal setting, monitoring output, and greater promotion of proven technology tools that increase productivity. Then the productivity paradox could end."

http://TheHRDirector.com, December 2, 2023

Is There a Better Way?

It's hard not to wonder where we might be today if Follett and Gilbreth had had their way 100 years ago, and the workplace had become a place where pursuit of profit was balanced with a positive approach to hiring, retaining, and training workers. What if goals had been more collaboratively set with worker autonomy in mind? What if CEOs had not pushed for bottom-line profits to enrich themselves and their cronies, and had instead used some of that money to invest in workplace learning and research so that they could be prepared for the future? And what if goal setting had had a proven science – not SMART or OKRs – attached to it that included measurement of the softer skills that Follett and Gilbreth had recommended, like curiosity and collaborative decision-making? And what if that science could incorporate the types of useful research on individual differences in character strengths, mindset, willpower, priming, and gender impact that could ensure that current goal strategies are cutting-edge, streamlined, and optimized for the twenty-first century?

There Is a Better Way

The good news is that the science already exists in Locke and Latham's goal setting theory, and it is universally acclaimed, but rarely included, in any of today's popular productivity approaches. Any success strategy must start with an understanding of their seminal theory, which ought to be required learning in every school in the world. It is so foundational that Chapter 3 is devoted to its elegant simplicity and examples of how you can use it, as well as some of the most daunting examples of what has happened when people and companies have reversed its main elements – "goals gone wild."

Bridging the Past with the Future

And the last piece of good news is that I believe my BRIDGE methodology is a comprehensive and structured approach that allows individuals to personalize their own goal pursuit by considering all the relevant factors that can impact outcome, like mindset, well-being, and motivation, and that does justice to the ideals promoted by Follett and Gilbreth. I will take readers through every step of BRIDGE in Part II of this book – Brainstorming, Relationships, Investments, Decision-Making, Good Grit, and Excellence – complete with questions and relatable examples and supplemented and supported with this book's resources. I think everyone will leave with a blueprint to achieve success for any goal you choose to explore as you read this book.

Is it audacious to propose this methodology as a woman without a PhD to my name, and without a grant from a major university supporting my work? Researching and writing this book has convinced me that the answer is "yes," but that my audacity is informed by decades of experience and the confidence to know that this book is important at a time when the world needs it.

The greatest breakthroughs in any field have only happened when unexpected elements came together, new questions were asked, and unusual ideas emerged, which is what I have done to conceive of and create this book. Celebrated cellist and humanitarian YoYo Ma believes in what is called "the Edge Effect," which is when unrelated concepts collide and a new force emerges like a musical style or a novel type of literature. I've also drawn strength from the stories of Lillian Gilbreth, who juggled raising children with purposeful work, and Mary Parker Follett, a fellow Radcliffe graduate (it became Harvard-Radcliffe during my time in Cambridge) who had the courage to put her own ideas into the world at a time when women didn't have the power and platforms that I now have available.

Both women also found a way to merge their many interests – including our shared passion for psychology – into suggestions about new ways to think about how to make a positive difference in the world, something else we have in common. In fact, Marty Seligman, my mentor and the "father of Positive Psychology," has charged me and all the graduates of the University of Pennsylvania's MAPP program to use our education to create a 51% tipping point of happiness in the world, something I firmly believe is more likely if we all understand and use more effective and scientific goal setting practices in our daily lives.

It took almost 100 years for sharp-eyed researchers to bring the ideas of Follett and the more well-known contributions of Gilbreth back to the world's attention where we can all appreciate the prescience and brilliance of their revolutionary ideas. I hope it won't take that long for the questions I've raised about the skewed nature of goal setting and my ideas to improve it to make a positive difference, but all I can do is throw my hat in the ring and give it my best shot.

CHAPTER 3

The Science-Based "Secret"

The 800-Pound Gorilla Everyone Loves

What if someone told you they knew a secret that could make your life happier and more successful? Would you want to know what it was?

Of course you would! And today is your lucky day because this chapter contains that secret. And unlike the runaway bestseller *The Secret* of the 1980s, this secret isn't one of magical and fantastical promises about how to make your dreams come true. This secret is the elusive knowledge I learned in October 2005 that had been in academic and management textbooks for years, but that hadn't reached the mass market until my book, *Creating Your Best Life*, was published in 2008. Fifteen years later, there are still only a few books that have shared this secret with the public, so let's make sure that you and those around you learn it now.

Ever since two researchers – Edwin Locke and Gary Latham – decided to join forces to look at how to understand the ways that setting goals could provide the right motivation to get things done, there has been universal agreement that their "open theory" first published in 1990, and continually broadened since then, is the gold standard for anyone looking to achieve success with their goals. In fact, a review of the literature on employee motivation for the *Handbook of Psychology* described goal setting theory as the top-ranked tool to motivate employees at work.

From Taylorism to Behaviorism

It's ironic that Locke's decision to study goal setting emerged from doing graduate work in industrial and organizational psychology, the field originated by Lillian Moller Gilbreth 50 years earlier, that had also been focused on solving the problem of goal efficiency. Locke's entrance into the field coincided with behaviorism, which couldn't have been further from what Gilbreth proposed. Her solution had been a blend of psychology, engineering, and management to create a human-centric workplace that would result in productivity and efficiency because individual differences were considered.

Behaviorism, on the other hand, disregarded a person's internal state and psychological makeup, emphasizing only what was observable – someone's "behavior." It further theorized that a person's actions came from stimuli in the environment, and that if you wanted to change that person's behavior, you would have to interject rewards and punishments to reinforce what you wanted from them. Their thoughts and feelings did not matter. B.F. Skinner was the loudest voice in psychology on the subject, arguing that "man has neither freedom nor dignity."

Although Locke wasn't concerned about well-being as an element in productivity, he challenged the concept that a person's thoughts and feelings would **not** impact a person's behavior. His basis for this challenge was that existing organizational research on motivation showed that setting hard goals resulted in high performance in the workplace, which said to him that a consciously set goal **did** change a person's behavior. If that were true, he concluded, then how a person thinks drives behavior, not vice versa.

The Early Seeds of Goal Setting Theory

Locke set about replicating that finding in dozens of laboratory situations with different goals of varying complexity. He zeroed in on why hard goals had such a positive impact on performance and concluded that hard goals needed to be specific to have the greatest impact, and that they needed to be "attainable" (which varied from person to person). Being committed to hard goals was also key because easy goals were not difficult to achieve, thus didn't demand much from the person in order to succeed. Additionally, he discovered that feedback was essential if a person were to continue to make progress or change strategies as needed. These results became some of the anchoring principles of goal setting theory (GST).

There was one unexpected finding that required more thought before it became accepted dogma, however. Pursuing easy goals led to greater satisfaction with oneself, which surprised the researchers because the performance on those goals was much lower. But the paradox was resolved when the researchers realized that hard goals didn't create as much happiness as easy goals because the wins were fewer, and it took longer to achieve them, which delayed gratification and satisfaction. Thus, hard goals ultimately resulted in more pride and self-esteem because in the real world, the greatest benefits go to those who pursue the hardest things.

Pulpwood and Productivity

While Locke was doing his work, Latham was learning about inductive methods in Georgia Tech's graduate school that could be applied to problems in work settings. His master's thesis was about the development of job performance criteria for loggers in the southeastern United States. Latham found that ineffective loggers differed from effective loggers in only one way: the effective loggers set specific goals for daily and weekly cords cut per man hour. A subsequent job at the American Pulpwood Association narrowed the best performance among loggers to those setting specific and challenging goals, not just specific goals. Instead of seeing their work as tedious, the hard goals had given these experienced loggers a new feeling of meaning, purpose, and challenge. He and Locke had now both firmed up a key tenet in what became part of GST: best performance in both lab settings and real-world settings only came from hard, high goals, not easy or "do your best" conditions.

> Goal setting theory defines a learning goal as a desired number of strategies, processes, or procedures to be developed to master a task. A performance goal is defined as a desired level of performance to be obtained. Both types of goals have highest outcomes when the goal is challenging and specific. Vague and "do your best" goals are unproductive.

There was one other area that Latham tackled because of his academic training in behaviorism that became the other anchor of GST. As a staff psychologist at the Weyerhaeuser Company he studied the impact of intermittent rewards to reinforce behaviors (think casinos and slot machine payouts) and determined that when a person is learning something new, regular and intermittent rewards facilitate learning. He also found that self-set hard goals reaped the same positive outcomes as assigned goals, provided that goals assigned to others were accompanied with an explanation and rationale for their importance.

A Courageous Partnership

Once Locke and Latham became intrigued by each other's work and started to work together, history changed. Instead of seeking attention or riches, they doubled down on consolidating their own and others' research, and narrowing down the most ironclad results that could have practical application in the workplace. They argued, synthesized, asked questions, and took a bold step that set them apart from other psychologists: they created an "inductive" or "open" theory that could grow and change as more was learned about motivation, mindset, and cultural differences.

In 1990, they published *Goal Setting Theory*, which they have continued to update and broaden to this day. In addition to Locke's studies on the benefits of setting specific, challenging goals to achieve familiar outcomes – now called "performance goals" – Latham brought his observations of what they called "learning goals," and how they differ from each other in content, approach, measurement, and outcome.

One admirer of the duo's scholarship and approach to refining what has become the top motivational theory in psychology is Gabrielle Oettingen, whose own research on "mental contrasting" added an important dimension to goal setting theory. She wrote in 2019 that the partnership was unique for three key reasons: their inductive and scientific approach to relying on observable results to develop their theory, their willingness to buck the once-popular opinion in psychology that "nonconscious goals" had no impact on goal achievement, and their close collaboration. "Rather than focusing on networking, arraying big names, or adorning themselves with influential institutions, they were concerned with discovery, solid methodology, and meaningful application of the phenomena they had discovered," she said.

Reading Oettingen's words helped me understand in a new way why GST is still relatively unknown when it ought to be one of the first principles children learn in elementary school. She was right. Locke and Latham didn't chase fame, fortune, and media appearances. They don't have podcasts, television shows, or speaking engagements on corporate stages. Their focus has always been on rigorous scholarship that can help real-world people set and achieve important goals.

Consequently, at a time when psychology research is being challenged because of replication errors, GST stands out as one of the most researched, tested, and validated theories ever developed, and it's also one of the most universally useful. Without media platforms and mass market bestsellers, however, Locke and Latham's goal setting theory has languished in the background of pop psychology and is still mystifyingly unknown. And even as I write this, a search of "Harvard Business Review" for articles on goal setting theory ends after three mentions. The squeaky wheel, as we know, gets the grease and these two men are not squeaky.

Goal Setting Theory

Goal setting theory is simple and elegant. On its surface it looks plain, but it is the nuances that give it power. Locke and Latham have written that they have kept the theory "parsimonious" for one reason – to make it understandable. I'm going to reinforce their definitions of performance and learning goals several times, along with examples of each type of goal, to ensure that every reader is crystal clear on their meaning. GST is foundational to the addition of my BRIDGE methodology, which can't make sense without the engine of GST, and getting the particulars right around the type of goal you are pursuing is the rock upon which you will build your plan.

Goal setting theory says:

- ◆ A goal is the object or aim of an action.
  - • "Aim" is something people want to do but do not yet possess.
  - • Action starts with the idea that the state or object is not present.
- ◆ There are two kinds of goals: Performance Goals and Learning Goals
  - • Performance Goal: A desired level of performance to attain
  - • Learning Goal: Desired number of strategies, processes, or procedures to obtain to master a task
- ◆ There are three ways to set both learning and performance goals:
  - • No goal or "do your best" (worst and not recommended)
  - • Low goals (mediocre)
  - • Challenging and specific (best)
- ◆ The higher the goal, the better the performance if the following conditions are met (moderators):
  - • Ability, knowledge, or skill to perform the task
  - • Commitment to the goal
  - • Feedback on goal progress
  - • Resources and lack of situational restraints
- ◆ The degree of success at hard goals is affected by (mediators):
  - • The choice to pursue the goal
  - • Putting effort in a certain direction or on a specific task
  - • Persistence in pursuing the goal to completion
  - • Task strategy

Locke and Latham described their theory as a model for a "High Performance Cycle" with the following steps and outcomes: "Specific, high goals with their moderators and mediators, lead to high performance, which typically lead to high rewards that in turn lead to commitment to the organization and thereby the setting of high goals."

Latham and Gerard H. Seijits also found in subsequent studies that if a hard future goal undermined a person's motivation, breaking the goal into sub-goals resulted in greater initiative and confidence around continuing to pursue the goal, a finding that was replicated by others, like Albert Bandura, founder of Self-Efficacy Theory, whose work is an integral component of goal setting theory.

Performance Goals Aren't Only About Performance

Too many of my clients think that all the goals they set for themselves and those who report to them are "performance goals." I understand the confusion because it sounds like anything that has a hoped-for outcome must be a performance goal. Based on the explanation above, though, a performance goal is something you already know how to do and there is little, if anything, left to learn to identify what you want to achieve and when you want to have accomplished that goal.

Think about the loggers cutting down trees who proved that specific and high goals always resulted in best outcomes. Although every logger was competent and had the resources to succeed, they were not doing their best work or feeling proud of themselves until a hard goal was assigned to them. Because there was nothing left to learn and they saw what type of outcomes they could achieve with specific, aggressive numbers, the loggers became able to reliably predict their finest hourly, daily, and weekly log count. This is what allowed the American Pulpwood Association to take orders that accurately matched their large inventory, which then allowed them to make more money and have more satisfied clients. This is an example of the "High Performance Cycle."

Here are some other common performance goals that you might encounter at work or in your life (all these examples presume you have already performed these actions):

- Driving to a location for work or another task on a familiar route
- Teaching a concept to a class that you have previously instructed elsewhere
- Reconciling a checkbook
- Flying a plane
- Making a favorite meal
- Studying for a test
- Having a one-on-one meeting with a direct report
- Performing a familiar medical procedure such as a hip replacement, delivering a baby, or doing a mammogram screening
- Giving a speech you've given before
- Cleaning a hotel room

When you need to accomplish a goal that is familiar and you already have the skills and knowledge to do it well, that is a GST performance goal, and to accomplish it in a way that evokes pride and best results, it needs to be "challenging and specific."

Cleaning and Checklists

One of my close friends, Peter, grew up in the projects of New Jersey, and to help his parents earn as much money as possible, he cleaned office buildings at night with them. Once he familiarized himself with the layout of each office, the tasks that needed to be done, the cleaning supplies he needed to use, and the details that would ensure that the clients would be most satisfied, he set a goal of doing the job more quickly and effectively every week so that he could add some of his parents' offices to his workload.

Peter created efficient work systems to avoid circling through the same areas twice, and he found that leaving the supplies for each job in the rooms where he would need them ahead of time cut down on wasteful movement. He played a game with himself to see how fast he could do the buildings he took on, and he continued to perfect his routine until it was as swift and high-quality as possible. His curious parents asked for a checklist of how he was getting his results, and once they adapted it to their own assignments, they started to clean faster, too, which allowed them to knock off earlier so that everyone could get more sleep.

> A study published in the *New England Journal of Medicine* in 2009 described the positive impact of implementing the World Health Organization's Surgical Safety Checklist in eight hospitals around the world. The results included reducing surgery-related complications by more than a third and deaths by almost half.

Another friend of mine, Denise, is a successful realtor whose business exploded during the coronavirus pandemic when mortgage rates dropped, and large numbers of families relocated for remote work. As her time grew increasingly fragmented, she hired people to help her stage the houses, design social media campaigns, and handle the closings. Now she tells me that everyone on her team works off checklists that they created and shared with each other at weekly company meetings to keep up with the dizzying workload and not drop any balls.

For example, Shelley, Denise's social media director, continues to refine her video editing skills and knowledge about the algorithms of platforms like Facebook, TikTok, and Instagram, and has a concise formula for how long it will take her to record, edit, and write each post before she launches the daily promotions. Denise evaluates Shelley's performance by the number of posts that go live, the audience interaction (likes, reshares, new followers), and the number of qualified buyers who inquire about the houses after seeing the posts. Shelley isn't just good at her job, but because she has an efficient, proven approach to creating each post and using audience feedback to refine her messaging, Denise can set challenging and specific goals for her and have confidence that Shelley will always come close to, or will achieve, them.

The Checklist Manifesto

In 2009, surgeon Atul Gawande published a runaway bestseller, *The Checklist Manifesto*, which reported on the many ways in which the incorporation of checklists had improved outcomes from deaths in surgery to safe building guidelines. Checklists are standard operating procedures for pilots and are used for pre-flight checks, takeoff, landing, and handling emergency situations. Many studies have reinforced their contribution to safety and elimination of accidents caused by human error.

Four factors are essential to the creation of successful checklists:

1. **Design:** They are concise, focusing on one specific task with the most important steps
2. **Cultural Acceptance:** Cultures of teamwork and the awareness of the potential for human error maximize checklist use

(continued)

3. Training and Implementation: Organizations that include training on how to integrate checklists into workflow are key to their effectiveness

4. Continuous Improvement: They are regularly reviewed and updated as insights and new developments create opportunities to make them better

As I have refined my use of goal setting theory with clients, I have begun to describe performance goals as "checklist goals" because it removes the confusion of calling them "performance" goals, and everyone already knows what a checklist is. In the above scenarios, all the performance goals that Peter, Denise, and Shelley pursued were suitable for checklists, and they all had time and date deadlines for their self-set high, excellent outcomes.

Checklists perform several other positive roles when it comes to goal setting. A well-done checklist that is limited to five–seven items can help you break down a familiar goal into a series of smaller sub-goals that can help a task feel more doable. As you accomplish each one, you can celebrate and see that you are getting closer to your target, which will make you happier.

Accomplishing them in order can also create an "if-then" leveraged effect that can automate your behavior (if I do this step, then the next step is clear) and make goal accomplishment more likely. Checklists can also be viewed as action plans, which research has found calms people down and eliminates ruminative thinking that wanders back to the uncompleted task. Checklists can also make a company's mentoring program more effective because a mentor can distill their efficiency down to a checklist to use in guiding mentees to more effective behavior. And checklists don't have to be regimented in terms of how you perform each step because individuals can bring their own unique touch to how they succeed. One of the funniest viral TikTok videos I saw this year was of a flight attendant who made every step of the pre-flight instructions dramatic and funny, which didn't just have everyone laughing, he got them to pay attention in his own authentic way!

The human brain cannot process too many items at once, and researchers have determined that somewhere between five and seven items is the optimal number for things like a checklist that contains steps to follow.

The Checkered Flag at NASCAR

In sports, fractions of a second can be the difference between winning and tenth place, or setting a world record and being off the medal stand. That's why people who are seeking excellence in their performance goals are always looking for a way to be more efficient in how much water they catch and cleanly sweep forward in rowing, how little their head moves while swimming backstroke, or how quickly they spring forward at the start of a running race. Every motion matters, so they scrutinize their races for the smallest imperfections to improve upon.

This was the case with Jeff Gordon, a NASCAR racer who was ranked as a great sports car driver, but who wanted to be one of the best of all time. He and his pit crew team already knew how to do their jobs – for example, refuel the car and change or inflate the tires during the brief pit stops – and they were a united group that was familiar with each other's personalities and work abilities. There was nothing they could put their finger on that involved learning something new about each other, the car, or Gordon – so they did not have a typical learning goal to solve, either.

The team knew it needed to find 13 seconds in their practiced pit stop routine somehow, however, because if Gordon could return to the track more quickly, he would gain 300 yards on his competitors and be more likely to win his races. But where were they going to pick up those precious seconds?

Gordon's NASCAR team brought in a consultant to help them identify missed opportunities during the pit stop and together they brainstormed possible solutions. Finally, someone suggested that they were losing valuable seconds shouting at each other over the roar of the car motor. They experimented with using new hand signals that replaced voice communications, and adding that small learning component to the team's well-oiled pit stop routine (a performance goal) was the difference Gordon needed to become a NASCAR elite for the ages. He retired from the sport in 2015 as the top-ranked driver of the modern era and in 2019 was inducted into the NASCAR Hall of Fame.

Learning Goals

I coached an entrepreneur a few years ago who had decided to leave a comfortable management job where her department routinely won awards for profit, efficiency, and low turnover. "Julia" had climbed every rung of this company and had reached the pinnacle of what she wanted to achieve there, so when she left, there was a big send-off. Everyone assumed Julia's knowledge and excellent work habits were the perfect training for her next chapter.

Julia put several years of her bonus money – as well as money from friends and family – in her start-up, which she and everyone around her believed would be a runaway success. But it wasn't. When she called me for coaching, she was about to throw in the towel. Despite working long hours, joining a Mastermind group for accountability, and being initially optimistic about her company's viability, she felt like a failure and was baffled that someone with her reputation and resume was missing all her goals.

As Julia described her background of previous success as a manager and star employee and compared it to the results she was getting as a solopreneur in her own company, I instantly spotted where Locke and Latham's goal setting theory could make a difference.

"Julia, how many of the goals that you set out for yourself every week are things you have done before and that have a proven checklist approach to accomplishment?"

She thought for a moment. "None. I've never had to make sales calls, go to conventions, and run a booth by myself, or find factories to make my products overseas. And I've never run a social media campaign but I'm trying to figure it out myself because that's the approach that has always worked for me before."

Dogged Determination Is Not Always Useful

Julia had nothing but learning goals in her new life as an entrepreneur, but she was treating them like performance goals that she ought to be able to accomplish by just trying harder. I explained goal setting theory and told her that she needed to give herself the space and curiosity to learn the ropes in her new life without time deadlines or self-criticism. I told her that learning goals could become performance goals with challenging timeframes, but first she had to find ways to be mentored into what she didn't know, or find places to learn quickly, so that she could regain her excitement about her business and achieve the success she had hoped for.

"You're not a failure," I reassured her. "You're just a high achiever who had learned everything you needed to learn in your last job in order to set high goals and succeed, and you just skipped over the learning part of this new life of yours by assuming that working harder would be the answer."

The next time I spoke with Julia she had gotten a mentor through the Small Business Administration to help her with budgeting and forecasting for her specific business, and she had dropped out of her aggressive goal setting group and joined a weekly meetup of entrepreneurs who were in the same business she was in and who were interested in sharing insights and resources so that they could all benefit. Julia is now successful, has kiosks in malls up and down the East Coast and she still thanks me for shining a light on the difference between learning and performance goals at a time when she was ready to give up on herself. Now she helps other new entrepreneurs to know the difference and she loves seeing the light go on in their eyes, too.

A typical learning goal might be:

- Cooking a recipe for the first time
- Driving a stick shift car
- Taking a foreign language course
- Becoming a parent

(continued)

- ◆ Changing professions
- ◆ Getting sober for the first time
- ◆ Adding new responsibilities to your job
- ◆ Incorporating artificial intelligence into your organization's productivity methods
- ◆ Moving to another country
- ◆ Getting married for the first time

"I Can Do It!" Muscle

As Locke and Latham experimented in field and lab settings "doing stuff" to understand when and how goals were most likely to be accomplished, they were intrigued that another motivational theorist of their era – Albert Bandura – had refined his thinking on what he called "Self-Efficacy Theory," and that it was nicely aligned with what they were doing. Bandura's theory states that a person with self-efficacy has confidence in their ability to exert control over their motivation, behavior, and social environment; this mindset became another foundational building block of how Locke and Latham improved their own findings.

I like to call self-efficacy the "I Can Do It" theory because it reminds me of when my children were small and wanted to act older than they were. "I can do it!" they would exclaim as they pushed my hands away and tried to put complicated Legos together without my help or tie their own shoes. Sometimes their confidence in their abilities paid off and they discovered a new skill, and sometimes they failed but they were eager to try again.

The payoff of the confidence that always came from tackling something they weren't sure they could do – but wanted to try – reminds me of Marty Seligman's new "Learned Mastery" definition. It's obvious to me now that all children spend years adding new skills – occasionally failing – to master their environments and thrive in much the same way shocked dogs learned to escape their cages. Adapting and overcoming challenges is the normal stuff of life that we all must encounter, and when we do so, our self-efficacy will grow and give us the willingness to set harder and harder goals.

Bandura's theory met with wide acceptance among motivational researchers because it had the same simplicity as goal setting theory, and even interacted with goal setting theory because self-efficacy is one of the moderators that predicts success in hard goals. Remember: Locke and Latham say that a person's commitment to accomplishing a goal is one of the reasons they can succeed, and that commitment is enhanced by having ability and knowledge, which builds self-efficacy. Self-efficacy also predicts the ability to come up with a variety of possible solutions to accomplish the goal, which is "task strategy" in goal setting theory.

Four Ways to Build Self-Efficacy

To keep it as simple as possible for our purposes, here's all you must know. Self-efficacy is a belief that you can do something you haven't done before, and the confidence to figure it out. Building self-efficacy helps with goal accomplishment because you are more likely to commit to high goals and figure out ways to accomplish them. Building self-efficacy can be done in four ways, and sometimes this is a muscle we need to build before we commit to big goals.

To develop the "I Can Do It!" muscle, you can:

- Have mastery experiences by accomplishing small goals (largest impact in building self-efficacy)
- Have someone you trust express their confidence in your abilities with phrases like "I believe in you" (Bandura calls this "a persuasive other")
- Observe a role model in your environment who is doing – or has done – what you are pursuing; learning from seeing them or talking to them gives you insight and confidence in your own abilities
- Remain calm in the face of a challenge instead of becoming anxious, and not experience some of the signs of nervousness and fear, like sweaty palms and shallow breathing

Many people say that a teacher or mentor who told them that they had the talent to accomplish something hard was the key reason why they eventually succeeded. This is an example of a "persuasive other" in self-efficacy theory.

Goals Gone Wild

In 2009, one of the most controversial articles I've ever read came out in "The Academy of Management Perspectives" to great fanfare. "Goals Gone Wild: The Systematic Side Effects of Over-Prescribing Goal Setting" the headline screamed. The opening paragraph was no less incendiary. The authors made a sweeping claim that while goal setting is "one of the most replicated and influential paradigms in the management literature," they went on to say that its value had been overstated and that Locke and Latham had overlooked the potential for fostering "unethical behavior, distorted risk preferences, corrosion of organizational culture and reduced intrinsic motivation."

Not content to strike fear in the heart of anyone using GST in their organization, they disdainfully warned: "Rather than dispensing goal setting as a benign, over-the-counter treatment for motivation, managers and scholars need to conceptualize goal setting as a prescription-strength medication that requires careful dosing, consideration of harmful side effects, and close supervision. We offer a warning label to accompany the practice of setting goals."

Wow! That certainly caught a lot of eyes, and because *Creating Your Best Life* had just been published touting the significance of goal setting theory, my inbox was clogged with emails asking if I'd seen it. "Will this hurt your book sales?" more than a few people asked. But book sales weren't my top concern. The problem was that this kind of article can set readers on the wrong path.

The Astronaut of the Deep

After reading the article, I knew that the authors had made the same error that many companies and managers make in their use of goal setting. They misunderstand the deliberate simplicity of GST and don't pay attention to its nuances. The authors also made the mistake of generalizing some findings about goal misapplications that had been previously flagged by Locke and Latham themselves, and the authors faced backlash for what Locke and Latham responded to immediately in a point-by-point rebuttal.

What I have found most useful from this well-known article is that the headline accurately captures that massive disasters have happened when organizations flip learning and performance goals upside-down and backwards. This is also the type of dynamic that can hurt individuals who set themselves up for disappointment and dishonor when they strive too hard for an outcome that they promise to others, but that they have no means of accomplishing by the appointed date.

One recent sad example of goals gone wild is Stockton Rush, an entrepreneur whose goal was to become the first person to carry passengers to and from the *Titanic* wreck on the bottom of the ocean floor, and whose last name ironically captured the errant spirit of "goals gone wild" – rushing too quickly to completion. An engaging, handsome man, he originally aspired to be an astronaut but wasn't selected for the rigorous training, so ferrying tourists to one of the most iconic underwater wrecks in the world became his professional focus.

Rush rhapsodized that he was becoming an "astronaut of the deep," instead, and pushed to get paying passengers signed up as quickly as possible. He bristled at the industry standards governing the safety of submersibles because he said they stifled innovation and prevented him from being in business more quickly. Rush's "innovations," however, were suspect. For example, he turned a gaming console into a steering wheel, and chose to use a type of metal that cracked under pressure as the protective sheath.

Professional colleagues warned him that his behavior and short-cuts were dangerous. Rush thumbed his nose at the sanctions, though, and changed the classification of his vehicle, the Titan, so that it couldn't be regulated. He fired the man whom he brought on to certify the Titan's safety, later suing him for defamation when the whistleblower wouldn't back down from his claims that the Titan was a disaster in the making. Rush continued to charge high prices to ride down to the *Titanic* but had scary near-misses that those clients later reported with a shiver.

The end came when Rush took a full load of paying customers on a *Titanic* journey, apparently imploding within minutes of beginning their descent. A father and son lost their lives, along with a noted oceanographer, Rush, and others who couldn't resist the lure of the deep. The accounts that came out in ensuing weeks and months about the ways that Rush had been determined to avoid accountability on all safety checks so that he could make money with the Titan were instructive. Like several other business disasters including the "death trap" Ford Pinto of the 1970s and the ill-fated Boeing 737 Max plane crashes, Rush had turned a learning goal into a public performance goal because of ego and dollar signs. If goal setting theory had been heeded, lives would have been spared and companies might have kept their reputations intact.

The infamous business implosions of WeWork, Theranos, the Titan submersible project, and Enron share several striking similarities as examples of "Goals Gone Wild":

♦ **Overhyped promises and unrealistic projections.** WeWork claimed to be a tech company that would revolutionize the way people work, Theranos promised to revolutionize blood testing, the Titan submersible project aimed to take tourists to the *Titanic* wreckage, and Enron presented itself as a pioneering energy trading company.

♦ **Lack of transparency and deceptive practices.** Deceit, fraudulent accounting, and lack of accountability were tied to grandiose claims designed to fleece investors, maintain inflated valuations, and prioritize growth at all costs.

♦ **Cult-like leadership and toxic corporate culture.** Suppressing dissent and encouraging unethical behavior were common in these entities.

♦ **Ignoring warning signs and red flags.** Despite numerous warning signs and red flags raised by employees, experts, or regulators, these entities arrogantly downplayed concerns until they collapsed.

♦ **Catastrophic consequences.** The implosions of these companies/projects had far-reaching consequences, resulting in significant financial losses for investors, job losses for employees, and, in some cases, legal repercussions and fatalities for those involved in the deception.

What's Missing?

Although goal setting theory remains the basis of my work and Locke and Latham's scholarship is rock-solid, the inevitable march of innovation, technology advancements, enhanced sophistication in psychology research, and the shifting dynamics between genders in power and influence across many cultures have brought about numerous findings that speak to the need for updates to how goals are set and seen through to completion. Locke and Latham always expected that their "open theory" would evolve to include up-to-date scholarship and fresh ideas, so my BRIDGE methodology isn't a surprising development. Years of pondering the acronym, testing my approach, and using it with clients has proven to me that it has a valid seat at the table in the goal setting world – and I also think BRIDGE is "stickier" and more evocative of forward movement than SMART or OKR!

In the next chapter, I will provide more detail about the thinking and research that undergird my belief that we need to be more specific and evidence-based in our guidance on how to prepare ourselves for successful goal pursuit. It will include how to approach brainstorming in better ways, why our relationships should be carefully evaluated, and how to identify decision-making biases that lead us astray, among other topics that we will explore in detail in the second half of the book.

Lee Iacocca was determined to make the Ford Motor Company competitive with the smaller European cars that were cutting into their sales when he became president in 1971. In a flamboyant effort to put his own stamp on the company, he declared that Ford would create a brand-new small car in record time that would cost $2,000 and weigh less than 2,000 pounds. The Ford Pinto was their offering, and it resulted in hundreds of fiery car crashes and disfigurations. Later it was revealed that the pressure to get the car on the market much faster than it usually takes to design a new car had meant that engineers had been pressured to sign off on a car they knew was unsafe. Ford's learning goal of creating its first small car had been sacrificed at the altar of performance goal metrics to get good press and fatten Ford's bottom line.

CHAPTER 4

The BRIDGE from Theory to Success

Goal Lessons Learned from Overcoming Bulimia

In 1984, I was a 22-year-old newlywed in my seventh year of struggling with bulimia nervosa, an eating disorder that had no known successful treatment approach at the time. Despite trying for years and throughout my time at Harvard University to leave the behavior behind, I just became more secretive and self-destructive and spiraled downward. It was only after joining a self-help group for compulsive eaters in Baltimore that I began to get better, one day at a time – a state of health that I have maintained unbroken for 40 years.

In hindsight, I can see that my triumph over my addiction was one of my finest examples in my life of using goal setting theory (GST) without knowing what it was. I set a hard goal, committed to it with a clear strategy and persistence through setbacks, and I used feedback and support from people who believed in me to do something that was not widely thought to be possible at that time. The role models and cheerleaders I surrounded myself with helped me to change the way I dealt with food and encouraged me onward as I achieved one day, then one week, then one year, and finally decades of recovery. My journey back to health was the subject of my autobiography, *My Name Is Caroline*, which was published in 1988 and was the first book for the mass market by a survivor of bulimia.

Although I was proud of my hard work and determination to overcome this challenging disorder, a woman once said to me that I couldn't keep what I didn't give away. There was so much wisdom in those words that I have never forgotten them, and they have given my life the purpose it was lacking at the time. For 40 years I have done my best to be an exemplar of long-term bulimia recovery who gives away the support, knowledge, and acceptance that others gave unselfishly to me and now I do the same with the knowledge I have learned about how to correctly set, pursue, and achieve big goals with proven science behind it.

The Universal Eureka! Moment

Goal setting theory was one of two research papers that became the bedrock of my newfound approach to goal setting and creating success. The other one was "The Benefits of Frequent Positive Affect" by Sonja Lyubomirsky, Ed Diener, and Laura King. This meta-analysis showed that – contrary to most beliefs – we only succeed in our goals when we are in a flourishing emotional state beforehand. We do not become happy because we achieve something; we prime the pump for success when we elevate our well-being first in a variety of ways, from practicing gratitude to having a regular meditation practice.

Like everyone else who reads this meta-analysis or hears its findings, I had an instant Eureka! moment in 2005 that gave me a new perspective on why so many of my previous attempts to experience happiness as the result of my achievements had come to naught. This research paper explained why I had been on a fool's errand thinking that being on the cover of a magazine for my book, getting good grades, or moving to a desirable neighborhood was the ticket to lasting joy and contentment (which had never lasted as long as I thought it would, anyway). What might my life have been like if I'd tried to amplify my well-being by investing in good friendships instead of primarily focusing on being a high achiever at school, or if I'd performed more altruistic acts of service instead of trying to swim faster? Would I have ultimately been more successful in all my endeavors and happier if I'd had the right goal setting formula? The answer was clearly "yes."

An Updated High-Performance Cycle?

Whenever I lead a workshop or work with a client on goal setting, this happiness meta-analysis is one of the first pieces of information I share, and the universal reaction is the same amazement I felt upon hearing it for the first time. People can't believe they've made the wrong assumptions about how they'd feel once they achieved what they had worked for, but the approach makes sense once they think about it. In fact, I've noted that people are forever changed by this knowledge, and as a result they have a completely different perspective on the right approach to setting goals.

As detailed in Chapter 3, Locke and Latham proposed the creation of their High-Performance Cycle that would instigate a domino effect of success. It began with proper goal setting, commitment, strategy, and persistence, and the result was higher self-esteem and happiness upon successful achievement of goals. Their multitude of experiments validated the framework, but my Positive Psychology education was yielding an entirely new set of perspectives on success that I realized was missing from goal setting theory, starting with the fact that happiness precedes success. In fact, when I'm leading goal setting workshops for companies, I inform them from the start that it would be unprofessional of me to talk about the topic without first addressing the ways in which they could boost their flourishing every day if they wanted to create the conditions for the success they desired.

Lyubomirsky and her colleagues have continued to add research findings that bolster the importance of looking at happiness and emotional flourishing as the key start to any goal setting. In fact, several of her most recent papers on happiness and career success have shown that the connection between being in a thriving state as a prime for career success is even stronger than initially thought. She and her colleagues have repeatedly found across a number of cultures that people in a flourishing emotional state exhibit many of the behaviors and mindsets that lay the groundwork for high achievement, including optimism, zest, gratitude, persistence, and creativity.

These findings have been some of the newest developments that have widened the lens on the factors that contribute to goal setting and success. That's why I believe the goal setting field is so ripe for disruption, and why this book is so necessary. Next, I will share what

I have found are the most important factors and research that contribute to building a goal setting mindset and creating the strategies that are most likely to succeed. The following sections reflect more updated ways to look at areas relevant to success, like motivation, mindset, environmental factors, gender differences, culture, and well-being. Many researchers have devoted their careers to advancing the scholarship in these areas, and although I will not be able to mention all of them, the most relevant findings to assist in using the BRIDGE methodology are included. This book's resources will also outline how to move forward mentally, financially, physically, and emotionally so that you will be well-prepared for all of the goals you dream about achieving.

Me at My Best

Positive Psychology raised the profile of the use of one's top character strengths in the pursuit of goal accomplishment with the Values in Action (VIA) Character Strengths Survey created by Chris Peterson and Marty Seligman. The free test ranks a person's character strengths from 1 to 24, and researchers have found that identifying one's strengths is a boost to well-being, but also that focusing on the creative and novel use of one's top five character strengths in the pursuit of valued goals leads to more goal success. Locke and Latham noted that having a strategy for goal accomplishment was integral to success, and this book's "Me at My Best" exercise helps to identify the conditions in which your top strengths contribute to success. This will give you clues to help you create an optimal strategy. The exercise uses the VIA Character Strengths Survey that is available at the VIA Institute on Character website at www.viacharacter.org and will take 15 minutes. I don't know anyone who doesn't think it is one of the best 15 minutes they've ever invested in themselves!

In the last few decades, several proven pathways to happiness have been identified, but they work differently on people, depending on background, culture, and unique wiring. Experimenting with these "wise" or "positive interventions" to see what makes a difference is the best way to start. In addition to knowing and using one's top strengths in new ways, other positive interventions include the practice of gratitude, volunteer activities, physical exercise, journaling, meditation or mindfulness activities, forgiveness, and experiencing awe. Everyone needs to find their own boot-up menu for boosting daily well-being; other activities that many find helpful include listening to music, spending time with loved ones, and tending to gardens.

Mars, Venus, and a Universe of Differences

It is only in recent times that findings that were once touted as a one-size-fits-all approach to success have been questioned for their suitability across different cultures and gender. The newest findings that challenge accepted wisdom include how to negotiate, dress, network, collaborate, self-promote, and use specific words in certain settings. Even esteemed researchers like Wharton's Adam Grant, whose books cover topics from grieving to gratitude, acknowledges that his bestselling business book, *Give and Take*, which said that a key element of success in life and work was being a "giver," not a "taker" or "matcher," had gotten it wrong when it came to generating career success for women. He admits that if the research had been broken down more carefully before he published the book, he would have written that women do not get the same benefits that men do when they are "givers." Men who give are accorded respect and brownie points, while women who give do not get those benefits because they are expected to be givers. And men who say "no" to giving at times are seen as people with strong boundaries while women who say "no" for the same reasons are criticized for violating the norms of generosity associated with femininity. This is just one of many examples that I will mention in subsequent chapters as factors to consider when choosing relationships that will impact goal success, how to get helpful feedback, and what surprising factors will figure into your decision-making.

Are You Happy for Me?

It wasn't until researchers began to study the qualities of friendships and the ways in which those relationships played a role in goal success that it became obvious how important it is to choose friendships wisely and to be thoughtful about how to navigate office relationships. Shelly Gable of the University of California, Santa Barbara, has studied this topic extensively, and she finds that other people's reactions to your dreams or good news can either bolster your confidence or cause you to drop your plans. She says that if someone fails to be curious and enthusiastic at the mention of your good news, they should be avoided as much as possible. Most alarmingly, in the absence of being greeted with curiosity and enthusiasm, a person can lose their excitement about what they are pursuing and might even drop their goal completely!

> Gable's research on Active-Constructive Responding (ACR) says that there are four ways to respond to someone's good news: Active-Constructive (curious and enthusiastic), Passive-Constructive (nice but disinterested), Active-Destructive (openly hostile and insulting), and Passive-Destructive (being critical with a smile or laugh). It's nearly impossible to accomplish one's goals in the absence of curious and enthusiastic responding because that dialogue creates energy that leads to an "upward spiral of well-being," thus laying the groundwork for one's success.

Catching Emotions

Although Mary Parker Follett pointed out in the early 1900s that goals and relationships were altered by people's interactions with each other, it was 100 years later that the research on emotional contagion emerged to support this observation. Nicholas Christakis and James Fowler revealed that behaviors and emotions spread in relational networks, and that people who quit smoking or gained weight created a "new norm" that caused others in their network to do the same. The ability to take large datasets and uncover new hidden reasons why goals succeed or fail is yet one more piece of information to consider in forming goal setting plans that Locke and Latham didn't have the tools to identify or foresee.

The Black Sheep Effect

Central to Locke and Latham's goal setting theory is "feedback." This assumes that the feedback is neutral and unbiased to measure one's progress toward valued goals. But when the feedback is impacted by social norms, it can be misleading and inaccurate, and can prevent success from occurring. For example, women have been found to get different types of feedback in performance reviews than men, so any metric of feedback needs to be scrutinized for bias if it plays a role in goal strategy. It's also true that women who are seen as ambitious or aggressive with their goals will be judged negatively because they have evoked "the black sheep effect" of violating typical female norms of being communal and caring.

The negative reactions from both men and women to another woman's goal pursuit can be both verbal and non-verbal, with women often displaying "ghosting" behavior of excluding or isolating a woman from a group because of her success. This type of feedback isn't just emotionally cruel, being shunned or ignored because of goal success also feels physically painful, so a woman who is unprepared for these challenges could fail without knowing what happened, especially if there is no obvious outward sign of being undermined.

McKinsey's 2023 "Women in the Workplace" report compiled with LeanIn.org reported that women's lack of support for each other was responsible for hindering success by some. One respondent said, "There are instances where women feel they need to distance themselves from other women to align with the predominant male culture in their workplace, which can undermine solidarity and mutual support." Another said, "It's important to acknowledge that not all women feel supported by their female colleagues. In some cases, there can be a reluctance to mentor or sponsor other women due to internalized biases or fear of being perceived as showing favoritism."

Another gender-specific challenge to goal pursuit that has only come to light in recent decades is women's "tend and befriend" response when threatened. While men get aggressive with a "fight or flight" reaction when someone appears as an adversary, women are more likely to turn to each other for safety and consolation. But if a woman's natural reaction to the stress of being shunned or attacked for having big goals is to need comfort from the same sex that has turned on her, it can evoke loneliness, depression, and a lack of confidence in "playing big." The popularity of the "Mean Girls" trope as an example of what women do to each other has kept this expectation and behavior alive, which must be considered as an important variable when it comes to feedback in goal pursuit. Gender differences in forming, pursuing, and achieving goals were not apparent when Locke and Latham created GST, but many disciplines now investigate gender differences in their findings, another reason why GST would benefit from a fresh look.

Are Vision Boards Dangerous Fantasies?

The husband-and-wife team of Gabriele Oettingen and Peter Gollwitzer is a tremendous addition to the goal setting literature. Oettingen's research on imagining success found that a person who spends too much time living in a fantasized future can begin to believe that they have made more goal progress than they have. She also said that using "mental contrasting" – seeing a desired destination first and then backing up to the present to create a goal accomplishment plan – is more effective than simply imagining a positive outcome and moving ahead without assessing possible challenges. Her work is reminiscent of the ancient Stoic admonishment: *Premeditatio Malorum* or premeditate the evils in your path and plan ahead for obstacles in your goal pursuit.

Gollwitzer's research on "if-then" scenarios is well-established. He said that a person's chances of success with hard goals is tripled if they connect two actions together that help a person do hard things. He added that being specific about when and how those conditions would occur was essential. For example, "When I walk into my office tomorrow, I will sit down and spend 45 minutes completing performance reviews." An added benefit: when a person uses the environment to trigger specific actions that make goal accomplishment more likely, it conserves one's willpower and mental energy.

The X Factor

Until the early twenty-first century, the words used for persistence were follow-through, conscientiousness, diligence, resilience, and "heart." Locke and Latham's theory emphasized a person's ability to withstand setbacks as a key factor in eventual success, but Angela Duckworth identified a new quality that could be even more critical: "grit." Defined as "passion and persistence in pursuit of long-term goals," Duckworth overcame criticism that grit was "old wine in a new bottle" by performing a number of studies that showed how grit was different from other behaviors, describing it as the "X factor" of success. Studies of composers, chess players, and athletes found that talent or hard work simply weren't enough to succeed; combining talent, deliberate practice, and grit, however, unlocked success in the most difficult goals.

In 2017, I published *Getting Grit*, which unpacked how to cultivate grit, and I wrote that it was composed of behaviors like humility, self-regulation, hope, passion, and persistence. While some of the qualities that compose grit can benefit from hardwiring (for example, girls are naturally more self-regulated than boys when they are young), I argued that a person can cultivate grit if the goal is self-motivated, and they create as many conditions for success as possible. Duckworth has agreed with my approach, noting, "I don't know anybody who has thought more than Caroline Miller about how to apply the scientific research on grit and achievement to our own lives!"

Psychological Safety

Amy Edmondson's research at Harvard Business School on successful groups found that they were distinguished by several factors including reciprocity in turn-taking, an openness to all ideas, a lack of negative behaviors (interrupting, eye-rolling, lip curling), and mutual respect. Mary Parker Follett's ideas continue to look prescient considering the popularity of Edmondson's work. In the brainstorming section of BRIDGE, it will be important to assess psychological safety if there will be groups involved in your goal setting and pursuit.

The Progress Principle

Also from Harvard Business School, Teresa Amabile looked at what workers said were the most important factors that made work meaningful. Their number-one response? Making progress on valued goals and not money, time off, promotions, or anything else. Progress on goals that were valued, and that the worker found meaningful, are now known as "The Progress Principle" in business settings. Once again, looking back 100 years, it's hard not to think about Lillian Gilbreth's call to make the workplace more satisfying by helping workers to make more progress more efficiently, and to value their efforts as individuals. It took 100 years to get back to the same place where we were 100 years ago?

Using BRIDGE Effectively

One of the most salient findings of using artificial intelligence tools like ChatGPT is that it's been found that the quality of the question prompt is what dictates the quality of the answer. My BRIDGE methodology is designed around question prompts that assist a person in identifying the most important variables that make a difference in creating a good goal setting plan. These questions will help you:

- **Brainstorm** every aspect associated with setting a specific goal;
- Evaluate the **relationships** you will and won't need to move forward;
- Think about the **investments** you will need to make in yourself;
- Discern what factors will matter in **decision-making**;
- Decide whether or not you have the **grit** to proceed; and
- Settle on the definition of **excellence** you are shooting for and the timeline that will match it.

Each chapter will fully explain the concept and this book's resources will allow you to track your process and progress. Goal setting is serious but it's also fun, so keep turning the pages and let's create your best life together!

PART II

Crossing the BRIDGE

As you prepare to cross the bridge that will help you turn your dreams into reality, you will need to use the worksheets in the book (copy them so you have more to play with), a favorite journal to write in, or a notepad so that you can do the careful work of putting together a winning strategy that is likely to succeed based on the answers and insights that will emerge. Don't rush through the chapters, thinking you'll get into action more quickly, and therefore be closer to accomplishing your goals, without doing each section justice. Each chapter is designed to build upon the information you gather in a step-by-step way as you consider the questions on brainstorming, relationships, investments, decision-making, good grit, and excellence.

You may want to do this work alone at times, and sometimes with a trusted confidante or a set of friends in a Mastermind group who can both challenge and support you, as needed. In the chapter on relationships, you may be surprised to find out that there is a surefire way to know who has your back, and how important it is to be surrounded by people who have the mindset and energy required to be a part of your winning formula. You might also need time to gather your thoughts and feedback from others who have seen you "at your best" to diagram your decision-making checklist.

The most important outcome of the work you will do is that you will be moving forward, armed with the right science to steer you efficiently without wasting time and energy on unproven approaches.

My goal is for you to thoroughly understand goal setting theory, and then how the BRIDGE method can take you from setting your goal to walking through a process that gives you the answers and insights to take deliberate actions that lead to success. Much of the knowledge and tools you will see here will probably be new to you, so you will need an open mind and the willingness to experiment. The zombie goal setting approaches that have hung around too long and that won't die – like "Law of Attraction" and "SMART" goals – will not interest you once you experience the power of the science I've woven together from numerous sources in a way that is easy to understand and use.

Anyone who has spent time with artificial intelligence tools from OpenAI, Microsoft, and Google knows that the quality of answers you receive is dictated by the quality of "prompts" that you give it. In the coming chapters, there are many prompts that will show you some of the missing gaps in typical goal setting approaches. I want you to build upon these BRIDGE prompts to construct your own reliable framework, refining your answers until you have created strategies that work perfectly for you, and not necessarily anyone else. It will be the difference between buying a suit at an outlet store and ordering one from a tailor who makes it to fit you perfectly.

And who wouldn't want that? You deserve what is in store for you when you finish with this book, so let's begin our walk across the bridge that will take you to your desired destination.!

CHAPTER 5

Brainstorming

The Habsburg Jaw Effect

When you mention the word "brainstorming," it evokes images of people sitting around a table for hours, throwing out ideas in the assumption that at least one of those concepts will be so fabulous that everyone will agree on a solution, and a problem will be brilliantly solved – something many people and organizations continue to do in a flawed attempt to generate solutions to thorny twenty-first century challenges. Business periodicals and other media continue to push this as a viable innovation approach, encouraging readers with titles like "Five Steps to Effective Brainstorming" or "Ten Ways to Generate Bold Ideas at Your Next Offsite."

This in-person approach – originally called "brain-storming" – was created by a 1950s advertising executive, Alex Osborn, who made it his life's mission to help people come up with as many crazy ideas as possible at the outset of solving problems in the hopes that there would be more innovation in the world. But recent research has shown that fewer ideas, and fewer good ideas, happen in these conditions – often derisively called "groupthink" – particularly when the people involved in brainstorming look like each other, know each other well, and have similar cultural and educational backgrounds.

I've found "groupthink brainstorming" to be so useless in my work that I've come up with a name to describe its ineffectiveness: "The Habsburg Jaw Effect." The Habsburgs were a royal dynasty that ruled Europe for hundreds of years, and to preserve power, they shunned outsiders and married each other, resulting over time in a facial deformity so hideous that it became known as the "Habsburg Jaw." Even worse, the inbreeding caused the line to end with King Charles II of Spain in 1700 because the generations of intermarriage had left him sterile.

The antiquated brainstorming approaches are identical to the doomed Habsburg line; when everyone in a decision-making process is similar, the results lack vibrancy and originality, and ideas are dead on arrival. The BRIDGE methodology's brainstorming approach, on the other hand, is designed to evoke curiosity about yourself and discover new ways to get things done by asking the right questions. Some questions you will answer alone, and some will benefit from the input of others who can help you devise a plan to overcome any obstacles and tripwires that might lie in your path. The types of groups you work with, and the people whose input you seek, though, must meet certain standards. Surprising research has shown that the words and attitudes of others can wreak havoc on our confidence and forward progress if we are not careful.

The simple act of identifying a goal does several important things:

- You immediately scan your brain for what you do and don't know about how to accomplish the goal, and quickly identify helpful resources and knowledge.
- Your focus is narrowed and anything that is pertinent to that goal is more likely to catch your attention while useless information is more readily ignored.
- It creates zest and optimism.

Premeditatio Malorum and Premeditatio Bonum

The Ancient Stoics, Greek philosophers who originated in Athens around 300 BCE, believed that curiosity was a powerful advantage in staying alive and achieving one's aims. Their rational, practical approach to life emphasized preparation, diligence, and perseverance in response to inevitable challenges. They preached *premeditatio malorum* – a Latin phrase – which translates into "preparing for the evils" that you will encounter when you are trying to achieve your goal. The Stoics didn't consider this outlook pessimistic; on the contrary, they were optimists whose preparation for the future often led to success.

The Stoic spirit of examining all variables to be ready for curveballs and surprises infuses the BRIDGE methodology, which is designed to give everyone their best possible shot at getting where they want to go by being scrupulously prepared. I have added a twist based on my training in Positive Psychology, though, by including a concept I call *premeditatio bonum*: prepare for the good that will cross your path, and not just the bad. Let's use these blended principles to demonstrate how they can work for you right now in two learning goal (something you have never done before) scenarios that are common in people's lives.

TripAdvisor and Waze

Imagine you are planning your first vacation to a foreign country, and you want to know best places to stay given your family's interests, what type of weather you're likely to experience, what tourist traps you should avoid (the bad), and which popular attractions you should book ahead of time (the good). You might also want to know if airfare prices are better if you buy early, or if you have enough credit card miles to subsidize some of the costs and not pay any money at all. How might you approach getting the answers to these questions?

Chances are you would look at a website like TripAdvisor or buy guidebooks from well-respected authors like Rick Steves to get a general overview of where you are going. You might ask friends if they have had any memorable experiences in those countries (the good), or if they know someone who has a cautionary tale about pickpockets or overcharges in that region (the bad). You could also talk to a travel agent to determine if that type of consultant is the right investment for you, and you could watch YouTube videos to learn more about the history of the country and get apps for your mobile phone that provide self-guided walking or driving tours. Being curious and open-minded to be better informed about your vacation plans will inevitably result in a better experience for everyone.

Think about another common learning goal. Imagine one of your children has a sports tournament at an unfamiliar location 30 miles away, and you have a tightly organized weekend with several other events to coordinate with your spouse. You don't know if you should arrange a carpool or juggle commitments differently, so you will probably input the tournament address in a driving app like Waze. That will tell you the fastest, easiest route to get there (the good) and how to avoid potholes and construction road closures (the bad). That up-to-date information will make you more efficient and prevent you from getting lost or being late. By crowdsourcing information through friends, listservs, and reliable apps and websites, we flatten our learning curves quickly and create our best days and experiences. This is the same approach we will often need to create optimal strategies for other goals that we set for ourselves. The principles don't change, but the scenarios do, and if we integrate goal setting theory and the BRIDGE approach into how we live, our days will be simpler and less chaotic, and we will get more done.

Stages of Change

I have spent years creating my step-by-step BRIDGE methodology, and if you follow it faithfully you will have a clear roadmap for achieving your goals. If you skip a step to rush into action, though, I've found that you inevitably must go back and start all over. This is identical to what James Prochaska and Carlo DiClemente found when they mapped their Transtheoretical Change Model in the late 1970s of the actions taken by smokers who successfully quit their habit.

Prochaska and DiClemente noticed that if the person desiring smoking cessation did not follow the model's "stages of change" exactly – pre-contemplation before thinking about change, contemplation of what must be changed to succeed, preparation for the change process, the action of changing, maintenance of the change, and termination of the change process – they always had to go back and do the step they had skipped. My BRIDGE approach is no different; give this chapter your close attention to lay your foundation for creating and following your strategy, and you won't need to retrace your steps.

Building the Scaffolding of Your BRIDGE

Before we can narrow down to a strategy for your specific goal, we must first zoom out to put your life into a bigger context. In organizations, this is often done by anchoring the company to its purpose, which emerges from answering the following questions: Why do we exist? What do we offer that the world needs? In one's personal life, the word that has become catchy in recent years to capture this spirit is the Japanese word, *ikigai*, or "that which I wake up for." Having a purpose was identified as one of the common denominators among "Blue Zone" individuals all over the world who lived long, healthy lives. Researchers have also found that adults who feel purposeful about what they do and how they approach their days are less likely to suffer from degenerative brain disorders like Alzheimer's and are more likely to remain cognitively alert and engaged in life.

What Do You Wake Up For?

As we begin to chart your strategy, let's start with your *ikigai*, or purpose. If you don't know what it is, stop and spend some time on a worksheet included in the book: taking the free VIA Character Strengths test and writing a "Me at My Best" essay. When done together, the results shine a spotlight on what you do and how you do it when you are coming from your best place. It's much easier to identify your purpose when you can see the threads that connect your top strengths with actions that have elevated your emotions or made a difference in another person's life.

For example, you might notice that you often combine top strengths of self-regulation and leadership to be a steady presence in a group during challenging times. That might lead you to see your *ikigai* as being someone who can bring discipline and a commanding presence to the lives of people who need calm leadership and structure. If you have top strengths of curiosity and judgment/ critical thinking, this mixture could lend itself to always making well-informed, thoughtful decisions, and that might result in people coming to you for reliable guidance. Taking the free 15-minute VIA test and then writing a "Me at My Best" essay is one of the most popular assignments I give to clients and organizations because of the lasting insights it provides, and as you think through your "why," it will be tremendously enlightening.

> "The greatness of a man is not in how much wealth he acquires, but in his integrity and his ability to affect those around him positively."
>
> *Bob Marley*

What's the Dream?

Once you understand your purpose – who you are at your best – the next thing to unlock is your vision – what you want to do. My favorite question to discover this answer is "What is the dream?" Research has found that using the word "dream" at this point of the strategy process can unlock a potent pathway of hopeful, empathic thinking that the word "goal" does not. Too often people associate the word "goal" with burdens or failed change efforts, so let's take some time to understand what your own dreams are, especially if you have never thought deeply about what you really want and what would make life meaningful.

> "Imagining the future may be more important than analyzing the past."
>
> *C. K. Prahalad*

Marty Seligman often reminded us in the MAPP program that one of the greatest gifts we have as human beings is the ability to "prospect" the future, which is trying on different "possible selves" to see what lights us up. Most people never invest time, effort, or imagination contemplating what they want from life, however, or what type of positive difference they can make with their individual gifts. In fact, a 2023 *Harvard Business Review* article noted that three consultants who offered public workshops on how to use business concepts to craft a life strategy found that only 9% of participants had identified their purpose and only 3% had created a life strategy, something I have also found in three decades of working with people on goal setting. It's easy to get caught in living a reactive life of responding to what is put in front of you, or that is left undone from yesterday, so working through the BRIDGE approach is a golden opportunity to break out of thinking small about your dreams, or not thinking about them at all!

A Glimpse Beyond the Horizon

My favorite exercise from Positive Psychology to unearth a person's vision and dreams is called "Best Possible Future Self," a worksheet also provided in this book. When you write about your life in the future as if everything has gone as well as possible, 3 days in a row for at least 15 minutes, elaborating as much as possible about where you are living, who is around you, what occupies your time, and what emotions you experience, your goals can become clearer and you can see that future self more clearly in your mind's eye. The journaling exercise can also make it easier to identify specific goals to use in your BRIDGE process, and that will help move you closer to your desired future.

This exercise is also a powerful way to unearth regrets around actions not yet taken to become your "ideal self." Researchers Tom Gilovich and Shai Davidai have found that we have a "trinity of selves" – our "actual" day-to-day self, our "ought" self, who does what others expect of us, and our "ideal" self, who is the person we long to become. Regrets about paths we failed to take to become our "ideal" selves cause the most painful feelings and writing a "Best Possible Future Self" essay, along with a plan to actualize that existence, can soothe our deepest regrets.

In 2018, when Sir Simon McDonald was head of the British Foreign Office in London, he started "The Mirror Challenge" to encourage women to imagine themselves holding one of the senior diplomatic roles that had yet to be filled by a woman. He was inspired by Dame Mary Beard's report of a similar mirror challenge in the Italian Parliament in Rome. In London,

(continued)

13 mirrors, each labeled with one of the jobs McDonald wanted to disrupt, run along a prominent hallway where women can stop and gaze at their reflection, along with the title of that role directly underneath their face. Diversity rose under McDonald and his successor. In 2020, Dame Karen Pierce became the first woman to be named ambassador to the United States – the most senior overseas position in the Diplomatic Service. Hers was the last mirror to be replaced by a picture under McDonald (the fifth). In 2024, when Lindy Cameron arrived in New Delhi as the first female British High Commissioner to India, the tenth mirror flipped.

Avoid Buridan's Ass

Another positive outcome of "Best Possible Future Self" is that it clarifies "goals in conflict." Sometimes we don't know that we are holding two important dreams inside of us, and one of them cannot be pursued at the same time as the other one because they "conflict" with each other. For example, we might long to start a family, but we might also want to go to college at the same time. Certainly, there are people who have accomplished both goals simultaneously, but if a lot of time and energy goes toward making ends meet instead of giving necessary focus to one or the other, it's best to decide that one of them needs to be tabled until the other one has been completed. Whenever this isn't done, the research shows that we stalemate and don't make progress on either goal. A fourteenth century French philosopher, Jean Buridan, captured this dilemma perfectly with his observation that a donkey that is both hungry and thirsty, but who cannot decide whether to eat the hay or drink the water that is placed on either side of him at equal distance, will starve to death. This doomed donkey came to be known as "Buridan's Ass."

WOOPing It Up

Some people find that dreaming 5 or 10 years into the future is too overwhelming, and they want to start smaller with their goal setting.

If you feel this way, one suggestion is to write a letter to yourself one year in the future, reflecting on the accomplishments you are proud of that you achieved during the year, what you did to make them happen, and who helped you along the way. A new finding by Canadian researchers might make this even more powerful if you add one more step.

Yuta Chishima and Anne Wilson reported in 2020 that studies of two groups of high school students found that those who wrote a letter to themselves three years in the future as well as a letter from that future self back to themselves in the present day, had a host of positive outcomes that students who only wrote a letter to their future selves did not have. These included more diligence about school assignments, more self-efficacy, improved delay of gratification, and increased career planning. This "future self-continuity" is powerful because it lessens the gap between the present and future self and creates more optimism about how to achieve the hoped-for future.

Their finding closely mirrors the research of Gabrielle Oettingen on the importance of "mental contrasting." Oettingen found that people are more likely to pursue their present-day goals with zest and optimism if they do something called "WOOP," which means make a WISH, identify OBSTACLES, strategize how to OVERCOME them, and execute your PLAN. As mentioned earlier, her conclusion was that when we spend too much time fantasizing about a desired future without also coming back to the present and creating a strategy to overcome obstacles, we become overwhelmed quickly and kid ourselves into thinking that our fantasized future is easier to achieve than it really is.

Have You Met Me Before?

Research has found that when you begin to vividly imagine, describe, and feel closely connected with your future self, it becomes easier to act proactively in the present to create that hoped-for future. This is called having "future self-continuity," and without that emotional arousal and felt connection, the studies show that you see your future self as someone else. This technique has been successfully used by financial consultants to help with retirement planning; age-progressed images of one's older self tend to bring the future into stark focus, creating a greater sense of urgency about saving money.

This finding even held true for rural farmers in Ethiopia, who formed "mental models" of their best future selves after watching a one-hour documentary about farmers in similar situations who had succeeded in agriculture or business efforts without government interventions. Six months after the screenings, these farmers had higher aspirations, saved more money, enrolled their children in schools, and were more likely to use credit to create opportunities for themselves. Seeing a possibility of what their lives could be and then returning to their present lives to make plans for change, had altered these poor farmers in important psychological and physical ways.

What Type of Goal Do You Have?

After you have used your curiosity to think about your purpose and your vision, and you have done some time travel to become friendly with your future self, it's time to pick a goal and learn how to BRIDGE your way from here into your desired future. Whether you used exercises like "Best Possible Future Self" to identify a goal, or if you picked up this book already knowing what big goal you what to accomplish, now we will walk through my BRIDGE process of change. Grab a journal where you can begin to create your goal strategy, or use the worksheet entitled "How to Go from Here to There" to start our work.

And We're Off!

- ◆ What is your purpose?
- ◆ What is your vision?
- ◆ Select a goal from "Best Possible Future Self" or one that is meaningful to you.
- ◆ Is this a learning goal or a performance goal?

Remember – a learning goal is something you are learning how to do for the first time. A performance goal is something you have accomplished before that will fit onto a checklist of steps that don't require a different approach every time you pursue that goal. If you have a learning goal, go through the questions below and write your answers as we go along. If you have a performance goal, skip to the "Performance Goals" section, and answer those questions.

Learning Goals

◆ What is the specific learning goal?

Example: Learn three self-defense techniques I can do if I am grabbed from behind.

◆ What is the knowledge I need to acquire and where can I get it?

Example: If you have been asked to sell something you've never sold before, think about who could share that knowledge with you. Can you learn what you don't know from online sources? What other resources are available to you? Alumni communities? Neighborhood email listservs?

◆ What are the specific skills or behaviors I will need to have or acquire to achieve this goal?

Example: Physical strength? Emotional stability? Eye-hand coordination? Willpower?

◆ What have I done previously that is like the actions or knowledge that is required for me to succeed now?
◆ Who has accomplished this goal before and how can I learn more about the process they used?

Example: Possible answers include a mentor, teacher, figure from history, Wikipedia, biography, YouTube videos, and case studies.

◆ If no one has ever accomplished this goal, what is the closest match to this goal that I can learn something from?

Example: If you are creating a sustainable product that won't hurt the environment that no one has done before in your area of specialty, you can learn about "green" production methods from other eco-friendly companies, or you can read articles about people who have tried and come close to achieving sustainable products in other areas.

- How will I make the acquisition of this knowledge "challenging and specific"?

Example: If you want to learn salsa dancing and you've never taken a dance lesson, a challenging and specific learning goal would be come up with a list of five places to learn how to salsa dance (watching TikTok videos, signing up for dance lessons, asking friends if anyone can teach you, etc.), and setting a goal to evaluate those learning options for yourself within one week. An "unchallenging" approach would be to "try to imitate salsa dancers on TikTok."

- What is my deadline for this learning goal and how often will I assess my progress to see if my learning approach is working?

Example: I want to give my first public speech in three months and every two weeks I will gauge how well I'm doing by using my metric of progress.

- What metric will I use to assess progress?

Example: I can speak for another two minutes every week without flushing bright red.

- Summarize your answers into a coherent paragraph that starts with the goal and weaves in your answers to the other questions. You should have a clear set of sentences that establishes the goal, how much you need to add to your knowledge or skills, where you will find the information to flatten your learning curve as fast as possible, and the metric you will use to establish if you are making the right progress. If you find you are not making the right progress, write your alternative learning approaches about how you can achieve your challenging and specific learning goal by the date you have established.

Performance Goals

Remember: a performance goal is like a recipe that is so familiar to you that you can fit the steps onto a checklist and use it to get consistent results. The checklist can also be used to teach someone else how to do something, like train them how to take over duties in your job. Writing a book is a performance goal for me because I have a checklist of things I do every time (this is my ninth book) and items I must have to achieve a book deadline. Of course, there are variables that might make my plan a bit harder to achieve on time, like getting sick or having a computer stolen (both have happened to me at inopportune moments on book deadlines) but I always arrange for long days in isolation, daily page counts, and certain organizational tools that never vary, like storing information in Evernote folders with multiple tags, and using sticky Post-It poster paper to cover walls when I am creating chapter content ideas.

- ◆ What is your specific performance goal?

Example: To finish graduate school on time or to turn in my income tax one month early to get my refund.

- ◆ Create a checklist of the steps you've carried out in pursuit of that goal when you've had your best outcomes.

Example: Look at the performance goal worksheet to get an idea of common performance goals, and what their checklists might contain. Although checklists usually don't change, there are always opportunities to experiment with some of the steps to see if you can get a better, or more efficient, outcome depending on what might be happening in the world or in your profession. This means that although there might be a tiny bit of new learning (recall how Jeff Gordon's NASCAR pit crew learned hand signals to reclaim 13 seconds and achieve a better performance goal outcome) that can occur with a performance goal, they are still considered performance goals, not learning goals.

- ◆ What is your "challenging and specific" outcome?
- ◆ What is the metric you will use to gauge progress?
- ◆ What is your deadline?

- ◆ Write a paragraph summarizing the goal, what you need to accomplish it, and make a checklist of the familiar steps you will take. Put due dates for the completion of the steps that will lead you to your challenging and specific outcome.

And There's More!

This is where learning and performance goals come back together so you can examine a few more questions to ensure that you design an up-to-date, successful strategy that has *premeditatio malorum* and *premeditatio bonum* included. People with learning goals might have already considered how to deal with some of the challenges listed below, but it will still be helpful to carefully work through these questions, along with case study solutions, to consider every angle of your goal pursuit.

What's New in the World?

I am constantly impressed by the nuances involved in successful goal setting, and that is what makes it so important to remain current with up-to-date knowledge that can enhance your goal pursuit strategy. This can include being on top of scientific breakthroughs that have changed how technology speeds up specific work, or if some of your required resources have improved in quality. To do this, it might mean being on listservs where scientists and psychologists share research on performance breakthroughs, or spending time with a meetup or LinkedIn group where people like you get together to share best practices and new thinking.

It's often said that one's battle plan never survives first contact with the enemy. Following are case studies to spark out-of-the-box thinking about how to both prepare for and react to unexpected scenarios that could impact your strategy.

"We Found the Needle in the Haystack"

In April 2018, a burly 72-year-old former police officer, Joseph James DeAngelo, was arraigned in a packed California courtroom and charged as the East Side Rapist, a notorious serial killer, burglar, and predator who had terrorized the Sacramento region in the 1970s and 1980s. Despite 44 years of meticulous policework and the investment of more state resources than had been put into any other cold case in California history, the crimes had remained unsolved until the advent of investigative genetic genealogy (IGG). Commented one detective, who marveled at the painstaking work done by forensic genealogists and amateur sleuths to finally solve DeAngelo's heinous reign of terror, "We found the needle in the haystack."

Pioneered by creative minds like CeCe Moore, a former entertainer and self-taught genealogist, IGG has now solved hundreds of cold cases like that of the Golden State Killer. Moore and others like her use crime scene DNA to discover distant relatives by combing ancestry databases with proprietary algorithms, rebuilding old DNA samples to predict specific physical features, and narrowing down suspects through carefully constructed family trees. The result of blending the fields of genealogy and cold case crime-solving has revolutionized policework forever and has brought closure to families who despaired of ever having answers to who had hurt their loved ones.

Beam Me into a Better Future

Even more lives have been altered – and saved – by combining the concepts of video gaming, augmented reality, and surgery to assist those most in need of surgery. Nadine Hachach-Haram, a reconstructive plastic surgeon in London, once made regular international trips to fix deformities like cleft palate or operate on civilians who were caught in a war's crossfire. One day, she learned that despite the humanitarian efforts of doctors like her, 9 in 10 people in low- and middle-income countries did not have access to basic surgical care. She felt like she'd been "punched in the guts . . . [and that her efforts had been] futile," so she decided to attempt to create her sci-fi "vision of a revolving planet dotted with operating rooms all around the world, all connected in a network."

Along with a software engineer, Hachach-Haram developed an app that allows surgeons to see and assist in surgeries, regardless of location. She raised money in 2015 and launched Proximie, whose web-based software permits surgeons to collaborate via live video streams during operations, and even beam their hands onto a patient's body to guide newer surgeons on where and how to make incisions. During COVID-19, the use of Proximie's software accelerated because surgeons couldn't travel or gather. Since more than 95% of the surgical sessions are recorded into Proximie's online library, surgeons can tag and notate surgeries for post-operation briefings and training. Hachach-Haram's innovative response to her frustration with the old "see one, do one, teach one" doctor training hasn't just changed and saved countless lives, she was honored by Queen Elizabeth with the world's oldest and most prestigious decoration, the British Empire Medal, for "extraordinary services by civilian or military."

- ♦ What if there was a science-fiction solution like Proximie to achieve your goal? What might that look like?
- ♦ What are some technological and medical breakthroughs that could help you achieve your goal in faster and better ways?

Enter the Black Swan

It was pitch black in the early morning hours of March 26, 2024, when a 684-ft-long cargo ship named *Dali* slid through the Patapsco River of Baltimore, Maryland, heading straight toward a concrete pillar holding up the 1.6-mile-long Francis Scott Key Bridge. Onlookers, some of whom had just safely crossed the bridge before the ship's Mayday call shut it down, helplessly filmed what happened next. Hobbled by a surprise electrical outage that robbed it of steering power, *Dali* slammed into the pillar and caused the entire bridge to collapse instantly. Six construction workers on a night repair crew fell to their frigid deaths.

The company that built *Dali* claimed in subsequent days that they could not have foreseen this occurrence, which quickly became known as a "black swan" event – something negative, rare, and difficult to predict, but that has a profound impact on history. Other black swan events have included the recent coronavirus pandemic, which led much of the world to shut down and isolate at home at once, and the sinking of the *Titanic* in 1912.

> "Nothing is so painful to the human mind as a great and sudden change."
>
> *Mary Shelley*

As part of our strategy creation, we must dedicate some thought to the possibility of a black swan event destroying our careful preparation to achieve our goal. Although many of the "What if?" scenarios that we entertain will be unlikely, the exercise of going through the thought experiment of asking ourselves what we would do if something like a global supply chain made delivery of all supplies impossible, or if the internet was rendered useless for six months because of a malicious virus on every computer in the world, will prompt creative thinking by you and others, and the results can give you the invaluable outline of a playbook to turn to at a time of dire need.

The Best Dressed Guest Has No Clothes

The following story is a useful look at how one company handled the black swan coronavirus event. Its agility in the face of unpredictable forces gives you a peek at the adaptable mindset and "why not?" behaviors that can salvage something that initially looks like an unmitigated disaster.

Abercrombie + Fitch is a well-known upscale clothier that caters to young adults with disposable income. This age group is likely to attend destination weddings that require several changes of outfit, from the night-before guest reception to the morning-after-wedding brunch. For many months, the company designed elegant but affordable jumpsuits, cocktail dresses, and suit separates that they planned to market as their "Best Dressed Guest" line. The advertising budget had already been spent and photos of attractive men and women socializing in warm locations were about to go public when the coronavirus pandemic shut down travel, weddings, and the probability of anyone buying party clothes anytime soon.

Instead of bemoaning their unlucky fate, the company's leadership quickly pivoted and committed to an entirely new, low-budget advertising campaign featuring the company's leisure wear. Employees were given cameras to take pictures of themselves wearing the casual clothes at home, where they alternated being on a computer with spending time with loved ones. The ads hit home with consumers who appreciated the effort Abercrombie + Fitch made to provide a realistic campaign that was honest and that featured employees who looked like them. If the company had been unable or unwilling to change direction and temporarily shelve the well-planned campaign because of the crisis (which they later launched with great fanfare when travel and party restrictions eased), the company might have gone under.

- ◆ Imagine that you woke up one morning and the goal you want to pursue must contend with a black swan event that changes the world as you know it. Write down five unlikely scenarios that would create serious challenges for you, and how you would deal with each one.
- ◆ How would your top five strengths help you to address these challenges?
- ◆ What good might come from this black swan event in the future that could make you or the situation around you better in the long run?

Will It Work for People Like Me?

One morning when she was young, my daughter, Samantha, was sitting on our bed watching me and my husband get ready for the day, and she made an innocent observation. "You match!" she cried out gleefully, clapping her hands in delight. I looked at her father and then I looked down at myself and we all laughed. She was right. My husband and I were both in navy blue suits and white shirts. The only difference was that he had a tie around his neck, and I had a bow.

I've thought a lot about that moment in the intervening decades, reflecting on how often I and other women have heeded the well-meaning advice to copy men if we want to be as successful as they have always been in the workplace. But that is changing. In an ever-expanding body of research, scientists and other experts are now concluding that giving women and people from other cultures the same advice on salary negotiation, leadership, public speaking, generosity, humility, and networking that work for men, we are set-ting them up for failure. For example, several years ago everyone was advised to be a "giver" instead of a "taker" or "matcher" because it was rewarded with reciprocity and leadership status. Unfortunately, the research has shown that women who "give" without strings never get the same benefits that men do, and when they say "no" and have boundaries about giving their time to others, they pay a stiff social penalty while men who don't give are seen as being strong and disciplined.

There are a dizzying number of ways that ambitious women with goals and who have achieved success will pay a price that men will never pay. Leading gender researchers like Madeleine Heilman have spent decades puzzling over why female leaders in male-dominated professions are judged more harshly than men, are not given credit when they do succeed, and are held to different standards if an unsuccessful woman preceded them. Even worse, if they do succeed, they are routinely seen as cold, self-centered, and manipulative, and the feedback they receive from both men and women can lead to social ostracism and emotional consequences.

Outside of the office, women and men are different, too, but in ways that are just coming to light. Women and men experience stress, make friends, play, ruminate, and age differently, among countless other physical and emotional differences. One recent study found that contrary to accepted medical knowledge, women even sleep differently than men do, leading them to perceive insomnia differ-ently. Raphael Heinzer, director of the Center for Investigation and Research on Sleep at Lausanne University Hospital in Switzerland, said with some remorse about the surprising finding, "We never make fun of our patients, but we didn't believe [women]."

Are You Hallucinating on Me?

Nowhere are gender and racial differences more obvious than in some of the earliest inaccurate output and "hallucinations" that have reportedly occurred in the large language models that have been trained to think and react by teams composed primarily of white men. This has led to a lack of diversity and a perpetuation of bias in some of the answers and output of ChatGPT and other artificial intelligence applications like Copilot, Midjourney, and Claude. Facial recognition programs have also been notoriously unreliable and often can't discern or predict differences between people. For example, there are reports that asking these programs to depict a beautiful woman will result in the creation of a fair-skinned, buxom, long-haired, thin, youthful lady in flowing robes, while a prompt for an image of a productive employee usually results in a white, bearded man behind a desk.

The algorithmic biases embedded in AI programs like OpenAI and Stability are so deep that prompts for Blacks have been depicted with pink skin, and prompts for images of Black women have included hairstyles with blonde braids. Even more concerning, a prompt in Replicate for a "slave ship" produced a warning on censorship while Midjourney said it would suspend the user's account because of the prompt. James Dobson, a cultural historian at Dartmouth, explained the lack of discussion of race in the early days of machine learning has left engineers struggling to overwrite the decades of input from primarily white engineers.

We Can All Grab and Go?

Nowhere was the mismatch between reality and absurdity more pronounced than in Amazon's proud March 2022 promise of a futuristic and simplified shopping trip at their Go stores. The ads said shoppers could simply walk into their high-tech Go stores, scan an Amazon app on their phone, put whatever they wanted in a bag as cameras whirred above them, and then walk out. *Saturday Night Live* couldn't resist skewering the idea that African Americans would have the same freedom and experience as white patrons who took a box of cereal off the shelf and changed their minds, or who filled their shopping bags with food and walked out without surveillance alarms blaring. The sketch featured a Black shopper putting an item he wanted back on a shelf while nervously telling the ceiling, "Uh, okay, I am putting the sandwich back, y'all!"

◆ As you look at where you are with your strategies, don't forget to ask yourself if the feedback you've received, or the knowledge you've gleaned, will work for someone who is your gender and who has your cultural or racial background. Talking to people who look like you or come from your background will give you an accurate idea of whether you should test your plan of action more thoroughly before committing to it wholeheartedly.

Example: There are many listservs and websites that feature the research of sociologists, doctors, educators, psychologists, and others who are clarifying findings or doing new research to see if previous assumptions and advice will work for many types of people. Although you may have to spend some time looking around for this type of information, it is so important in the execution of a successful goal plan that you should factor this into your due diligence. Some people join Mastermind groups that have members like them who can provide wise advice for these types of situations, and many websites are devoted to exploring what it's like to work at certain companies given your race, gender, or background.

You Are Now on Your Way

At this point, you should have written down your goal and answered the questions about how to define it and gather the information you need to succeed. You have anchored your goal with an outcome date, and you have looked at variables like cultural or gender bias and black swan events to think more deeply about the "what if?" scenarios you want to be prepared for as you set out on your goal journey. Now we will move to a key area that can make or break your goal – the relationships you need, and don't need, in order to improve your success chances.

CHAPTER 6

Relationships

Do You Believe in My Dream?

When Dara Torres, an American sprint freestyler, was training for the 2008 Beijing Olympics, she formed a bubble around herself consisting almost exclusively of the people who believed that she had a chance to win the Olympic 50-m freestyle event at the age of 41. Torres was daring to go where no one had ever gone before with her ambitious effort to redefine what was possible at an age that most people thought was over the hill. Torres knew that pulling off this improbable feat would only be possible if she engineered everything in her life to tilt her toward success.

One of the most surprising rules she set in the years preceding the United States Olympic Trials, which was where she would need to place in the top two finishers in the country – already a difficult task, but necessary to even have the ability to go to the Olympics – was that no one was allowed in her presence to distract her from her audacious goal unless they believed that she could win the Olympics. And that meant that her own father, who thought she was wasting her time swimming instead of being a full-time mom for her young daughter, wasn't allowed in the bubble.

Although it might seem extreme, Torres knew from decades as one of the country's most elite female swimmers that her physical conditioning was just one factor in the success she was chasing. She had finally beaten the eating disorder that had dogged her for decades and she knew she had to take care of her mindset if she'd have any shot at making history.

And she did just that – and more. Torres stunned the swimming world in June 2008 by making the US Olympic team as one of their two 50-m freestyle sprinters, then shattered historical precedent two months later by finishing second at the Olympics by one one-hundredth of a second. Torres is the only female swimmer to make five Olympic teams, and her gutsy goal pursuit forever changed assumptions about the age at which a woman must hang up her racing goggles.

> Torres is a great example of why SMART is not the right acronym to guide everyone's goal pursuit. What she was seeking was so unprecedented – not simply "attainable" or "realistic" – that she changed the aspirations of millions of female swimmers who suddenly could imagine themselves competing and improving well into adulthood – just like male swimmers had always been able to do.

The Heliotropic Effect

As we fill in the relationships part of our BRIDGE goal strategy – identifying the people we will need as well as the ones we want to avoid – we will explore questions about who evokes the best in us, and who does not. Knowing who the good people are, and what we can do to protect ourselves from the damage of bad relationships, is a rarely discussed, but vitally important, component of goal success.

Dr. Barbara Fredrickson, a noted Positive Psychology scholar at the University of North Carolina and the winner of many awards for her pioneering research on happiness, was the first person to draw my attention to "the heliotropic effect," and how important it is to be in the presence of people who have the same impact on us that the sun (helios in Greek) has on plants. She observes that all plants turn toward the sun and its lifegiving warmth so they can grow and thrive, which is beautifully embodied in the summertime sight of a group of sunflowers that are all facing in the same direction. As human beings we naturally perform the same action; we turn toward the people who make us feel the warmth and sunlight of their approval, love, and caring, and knowing who they are – and who they are not – is a first step in taking stock of the role of BRIDGE relationships.

Questions to consider:

◆ Whose presence and interaction with you cause you to feel more positive and hopeful – the heliotropic effect?

◆ Are there people around you who have that impact on you right now, or do you need to build in time to connect more frequently with people who do evoke that in you?

◆ Who has the opposite effect on you and how often do you experience interactions with people – often known as "black holes" – like that?

◆ What will you do to contain your time and energy to avoid being depleted by black holes while pursuing your goals?

◆ For whom would you say that you provide the heliotropic effect?

Catalysts and Nurturers

Teresa Amabile of Harvard Business School and Steven Kramer changed the minds of many leaders about how to cultivate a happy, engaged, and productive workplace when they published 15 years of their daily diary findings from 238 knowledge workers about their "inner work life." They concluded that the single most important factor that predicted a "good day" at work was whether they had made progress on a meaningful goal. This research has become known as "The Progress Principle."

Amabile and Kramer rejected the idea that difficult, stressful work challenges caused burnout and disengagement. On the contrary, they found that when the workers were pursuing goals that they knew were meaningful to the organization, and they had the support and resources to pursue those goals, a "good day" was when they had a breakthrough or saw progress on their goals. They were less interested in recognition or financial incentives, which surprised the managers who had been surveyed about the most important factors in terms of motivation or well-being.

Two types of people had the power to generate the "good days" that evoked creativity, team harmony, and intrinsic motivation: "catalysts" and "nourishers." Catalysts were the people and groups that provided direct support for the workers, and nourishers gave displays of respect and words of encouragement. "Bad days" often were triggered by "inhibitors" and "toxins," who were the people who did not take supportive actions, or who actively undermined progress.

- ◆ Who are the catalysts and nourishers whose support helps you with goal progress? Do they know about your big goal?
- ◆ Who are the toxins and inhibitors? What can you do to wall off their impact on your motivation and mood?

The Power of the First Responder

Shelly Gable at the University of California, Santa Barbara, has researched the impact that relationships have on our well-being, confidence, and goal pursuit. One of her studies found that sharing a big dream with another person might not be a good idea if that person isn't what is called an "Active-Constructive Responder" (ACR). Someone who exhibits ACR responds to our goals and successes with curiosity and enthusiasm and doesn't change the subject or undermine us. We always want to be surrounded by people who have this type of outlook – and we need to do it for others, as well. When you are pursuing big goals, or telling others about your hopes and dreams, don't ever forget that the first person's response will have an oversized impact on how you see yourself and the importance of that goal. And even more powerful to consider: Gable found that if the first responder's reaction is not an ACR comment, we are likely to abandon our goal within the following two weeks after our unsettling interaction with them.

Gable has found that there are four ways that people respond to other people's good news:

1. Passive-Constructive: ignoring the news and changing the subject

2. Passive-Destructive: smiling while noting that other people have not succeeded in that type of endeavor before, but that perhaps you will

3. Active-Destructive: responding that you will never be successful because you don't have what it takes based on your history

4. Active-Constructive: curious, enthusiastic, and excited to hear more about your news

Gable advises that the last response is the only right response if you are trying to figure out who your friends are and who you should stay away from – regardless of the position they occupy in your family or close friend group.

What Are You Catching?

Although everyone has heard the saying "Birds of a feather flock together," it wasn't until the early 2,000s that Nicholas Christakis and James Fowler published the research on social contagion that proved it. The two men took a well-known dataset – the Framingham Heart Study – and looked at the changes that occurred in people's lives when they altered their health behaviors. They found that clusters of contagion appeared when a person did something like quit smoking or gain weight, demonstrating that once a person created a new "norm" among their closest connections, that behavior became more acceptable, and it spread. So, if Uncle Andy quit smoking, it became more likely that his closest family members and friends would do the same. This is why many people, including Dara Torres in her quest to make Olympic history, are zealous about keeping negative people away when they are focused on accomplishing a big goal. Once one person's negativity enters an environment, it can become a contagious hurricane that infects everything in its path.

Subsequent research on relationship interactions has found that many behaviors are contagious, including happiness, sadness, grit, and even suicide. Not only must we know who does and doesn't have our best interests at heart, we also need to think about the behaviors we might "catch" if we put ourselves in situations that are counterproductive to our goals. For example, being in a college rooming group of heavy drinkers who like to party every night won't be a positive step if we want to join the on-campus Reserve Officers' Training Corps (ROTC) unit to help pay for college expenses. And if your neighborhood Sunday night mahjong game is made up of women who have narrowed down their adventurousness to changing their lipstick, you might want to find a different circle that has a bit more zest and curiosity about what their future might hold.

♦ What behaviors or attitudes do you spot in those you frequently encounter and what can you do to limit your exposure to these negative or counterproductive interactions?

Many women struggle with eliminating or putting containers around the negative people in their lives. Research has shown that women are raised to act sweet and have "best friends," but at the same time, women's tendency to wound other women with words and silence (also known as "ghosting") is one of the earliest weapons they learn to wield against each other, and often for no apparent reason. As a result, as many as 84% of women admit to having "frenemies" (friends who are enemies) in their close circle because they don't want to create dissension by rocking the boat. At the same time, ubiquitous cultural primes constantly remind women that "mean girl" behavior is the norm, including Mean Girl International Delight coffee creamer and a television series called *Mean Girl Murders*!

A World Record at 99

In 2014, I was competing in the United States Masters Long Course Swimming Championships when I saw something that awed and inspired me in unexpected ways. I was standing on the pool deck with team members, restlessly passing time until my next event, when I felt a hush coming over the natatorium. I glanced at the starting blocks to see why everyone was looking in that direction, which is when I saw a spritely older lady get out of a plastic lawn chair and hop into the pool, surfacing with a big smile and one hand on the tiled wall.

"This is the start of the women's 50-m freestyle," the announcer barked. "On your mark, get set, go!"

Seven women of all ages dove off the blocks as the older lady ducked under the water's surface and then pushed off, methodically stroking her way down the length of the pool.

The crowd clearly knew who she was even though I didn't, because the din around me got louder and everyone had risen to their feet, clapping and screaming in support.

"Who's that?" I asked a teammate as I took in the pulsing energy and excitement around me.

"That's Annie Dunivin of Georgia Masters, and she's probably going to set a world record right now. In fact, she's the high point woman of the entire meet so far."

Open-mouthed, I turned back to watch Dunivin, who kept up the same steady pace while the crowd whistled its encouragement and stomped its feet. All seven members of her heat had already finished and were still in the pool – also cheering for her – when her hand touched the wall amidst deafening applause. Dunivin, competing in the 95 to 99-year-old age group at the age of 99, did set a world record that afternoon, and after a big grin and wave to the appreciative audience, was enveloped in a towel by her 70-something daughter, who ushered her back to her team area to await her next event. Later I found out that Dunivin was a relative novice to the sport, and had only begun swimming in her 90s because "she didn't want to be bored."

I never met Dunivin personally, but simply watching her that afternoon and seeing the reaction of others to her joyful attitude about competing in her 90s rubbed off on me. She made me want to be a better, less stressed competitor and person, and instead of focusing on my own results that day, she changed my perspective and gave me a glimpse of what my future could look like if I lived with the same exuberance and open-minded curiosity. Even though watching Dunivin break a world record happened years ago, the heliotropic effect of witnessing this nonagenarian's zest continues to inspire me today.

♦ What behavior, skills, and mindset do you want to "catch" or reinforce from your environment that will help you accomplish your goals? Where can you spend time with people who make you want to become a better person?

Mind Mapping Your Future Web

I was walking along the shores of the Atlantic Ocean with a CEO client one balmy spring afternoon when I challenged the woman to articulate the biggest goal she could think of that would align with her company's mission and nudge the world in a more peaceful direction. She broke out into a big smile and then started to map out one of the most audacious missions I'd ever heard. She excitedly expanded upon her idea while we walked for the next hour, and when we got back to my beach house, we put a large sticky poster sheet on the wall so she could map out who she would need to know to pull it off.

Mind mapping the web of relationships that will play a role in your goal pursuit is always a powerful exercise. In this case, my client drew a circle in the middle of the page and named the countries she wanted to include in her dream at the end of each spoke. Smaller spokes were drawn along the longer spokes with the names of government officials, innovators, and scientists she either knew or wanted to meet. She added the names of colleagues and members of her board of directors next to anyone she thought they had access to, and over the next day we returned to this mind map several times, adding and subtracting, writing down what the "ask" would be, and further refining this huge dream.

That mind map is now a central touchstone of our weekly calls, and whenever she speaks at a conference or goes on a trip, she consults the map to see if she can meet with the names that correspond with that country or region. Because we were so thorough and the mind map was anchored to a meaningful dream, it has become easier for her to turn down speaking invitations and appearances that don't match her big goal, which is streamlining her time and not depleting her energy.

◆ Visual thinkers love drawing mind maps with different colors, so creating a large mind map of your goal and the people who could play big roles or be your support system could be a fun exercise to try. How might drawing pictures and using colors bring more clarity and fresh thinking to your goal planning?

How I Found My Own Missing Links

When I was writing my first book, *My Name Is Caroline*, an autobiography about my successful triumph over bulimia, I was a novice in the book world. I was 24 and all I had was a burning ambition to tell a hopeful story of recovery. I had always had the dream of being a writer because I loved to read and I instinctively put sentences together regardless of what I was doing, constantly rearranging words in my head and looking for the smoothest, most graceful way to express myself whatever the situation. But having a dream and knowing I could write a good story was not the same as knowing what to do to get a book published.

My Eureka! moment happened one day when I was reading a story about one of the movie stars in the so-called "Brat Pack", Ally Sheedy. It discussed Sheedy's battle with bulimia and described her mother, Charlotte Sheedy, as a literary agent in Manhattan. Since I didn't know any book agents or even where to find them, I took a chance and wrote Charlotte a letter (and even sent it through the US mail with a postage stamp!), describing my book idea and asking if she would represent me. Within two weeks I was on a train to New York City, where Charlotte Sheedy met me in the lobby of her apartment building and agreed to represent me.

Several months after I signed a contract with her, an auction broke out between several publishing houses that were interested in my story. *My Name Is Caroline* was published in 1988 by Doubleday, and for almost 40 years it has continued to give hope to suffering bulimics, along with its sequel, *Positively Caroline*. Sometimes I wonder what would have happened if I hadn't had the Chutzpah to write Ally Sheedy's mother out of the blue, but anyone who has a big dream understands what possesses us when we know we have nothing to lose and everything to gain from seeing who might be willing to be an important link or resource for us.

◆ If you knew failure wasn't an option, who would you reach out to for help in accomplishing your big goal?

Making a List and Checking It Twice

My story is a reminder that we will probably want to find people we don't yet know who can help us achieve our goal, and that sometimes we will have to reach out and take a chance at getting to know someone who might appear to be out of reach. If we are in search of a mentor or someone to give us advice, it's important to have done a lot of homework on that person so that when you reach out, you don't waste their time asking them for assistance with something that is easily found elsewhere.

Here is a suggestion if you want an informational interview or email exchange with someone who would be a positive relationship for you:

I am regularly contacted through email and LinkedIn to answer questions about how to publish a book, whether people should apply to the Masters of Applied Positive Psychology Program at the University of Pennsylvania, and how to get paid for speaking publicly. While I believe that you "can't keep what you don't give away," I want to give away the support and information that will have the greatest positive impact on the person who wants my help, so I ask them to take certain helpful steps.

I suggest they go through my website and read or listen to the interviews I've given, and discover something unique in my experience that they won't easily find elsewhere. While this requires that people do a bit of homework before we interact, it ensures that they will get the best possible knowledge that only I can offer. This approach is increasingly popular among busy people who don't want to live cloistered lives away from the public, but who must draw clear boundaries around their time so that they can do their special work without becoming depleted.

In spite of the clarity of my request, others' reactions to my conditions for connecting have been surprising; only two people have ever taken the time to hone their questions and do their homework before reaching out again. I've regretfully concluded that most people simply want to chat in general terms without focusing on how to learn specific things from me, and it has left me wondering how many goals haven't been accomplished simply because people didn't want to do the work required to benefit from a relationship with someone who can be helpful – and who is willing to be of service!

◆ Who do you know – or want to know – who has important information or a unique perspective that will help you accomplish your goal? If you don't know them, what is your plan to try to connect with them?

◆ If you are spearheading an initiative in an organization or group, whose support do you need to succeed, and who needs to be notified about your efforts so that you don't work at cross purposes with anyone else?

Example: You are a division chief, and you need the support of another department head or other senior leaders in your company to succeed at an important objective. Write down who they are and when you would need to notify them about your goal or get their buy-in and support for your own efforts.

Also consider:

◆ Is there someone in your organization who is great at listening and giving advice who might want to join you for a meal or coffee to flesh out or challenge your thinking?

◆ Do you have a mentor or coach who is invested in helping you? Is this something you would benefit from? If so, who has positively experienced those relationships who could share how that process helped them?

Who Has Your Back?

At the age of 11, a precocious singer journeyed to Nashville with her mother to submit demo tapes of her singing Dolly Parton and Dixie Chicks cover songs. No one was interested in working with this preteen girl, so she went home disappointed, but determined to focus on adding whatever skills she needed. At 12, a computer repairman changed her life when he taught her how to play the guitar. This allowed her to marry her gift for telling stories in memorable melodies to playing and performing her own music. By 13, the still-young Taylor Swift inked her first development deal and the family moved from New Jersey to Tennessee to accommodate her promising career.

Swift's meteoric rise to success and stardom is now legendary. She was one of the first artists to sign with Big Machine Records, and within a few years had released *Fearless*, which is the most awarded country music album of all time. At this writing Swift has the most number-one albums of any female artist, the most US single chart entries for a female artist, and the highest grossing music tour ever, among dozens of other awards and accolades. She was even named *TIME* magazine's 2023 "Person of the Year" for her multi-varied impact on the world.

Like many other artists who have been preyed upon by record labels and people who want to enrich themselves off their work, Swift has also been the victim of the dark, mercenary side of the music business, which is where her devoted fans, the Swifties, have had her back and helped her to change many unfair practices. For example, when Big Machine sold her master recordings and left Swift without artistic control or ownership of her songs, the Swifties bought her re-recorded masters and made sure that she had the weight of public opinion and financial support behind her.

People who have studied the phenomenal power of the Swifties to impact everything from improving the sales practices of Ticketmaster (whose website crashed when 2.4 million tickets were sold on the first day Swift's Eras tour was announced) to stimulating the economies of the cities and countries she visits during her concert tours, say the intense fandom is partly due to Swift's demonstrated commitment to, and interest in, her fans from the onset of her career. Her hand delivered "Swiftmas" gifts to fans and other generous gestures are well-known and contagious; the family of a Swift fan who was killed by a drunk driver after leaving one of her concerts received $125,000 from fellow Swifties who often donated in amounts of $13, Swift's favorite number.

The Ability to Love Others and Be Loved Back

In the Values in Action (VIA) Character Strength Survey's definition of "love," Dr. Chris Peterson, one of the survey's creators, frequently told my Masters of Applied Positive Psychology (MAPP) class that he had written the strength as "the ability to love and be loved back" for the very reason we see evidenced in the Swifties. When you are in relationships where you see yourself as the person who is doing the loving, but not as someone who is also capable or worthy of receiving love back, that emotion is a weakness, not a strength. To foster positive relationships, especially the ones we need as our own support systems, and as the soft places that cushion us in our difficult moments, we must be comfortable giving and receiving the warmth, kindness, and type of love that undergirds the durable bonds of authentic friendship.

♦ Do you have a crowd of supporters like the Swifties who would be there for you in times of need? If not, can you begin to use the strength of "love and be loved back" to create that type of energy? And if yes, do you also join with others to support people who need your help when they pursue their own big goals, or when they hit a speedbump?

When Shalane Flanagan, an elite runner who had been one of the country's top running prospects for years, won the New York City Marathon in 2017 – the first US woman to win in 40 years – the newspapers didn't just report her victory, they described what is now called "The Shalane Effect." Flanagan had gathered all her competitors and other female runners with big goals to share her training site in Oregon in the years preceding the marathon, and she cultivated an environment where when the runners were injured, she made sure they got the right treatment. When they were discouraged, she reminded them of their dreams and talents. "The Shalane Effect" describes the impact Flanagan had on every runner who joined her, as they all ultimately achieved success by doing best times and winning Olympic and World Championship races.

Building a Strong Bridge

As we move through the BRIDGE system, we have now completed the Brainstorming and Relationships steps that pertain to identifying and refining your specific goal and bringing into focus the relationships that you know you will need in order to succeed, the relationships that you want to keep at a distance, and the different ways that the heliotropic effect can make you productive, engaged, and optimistic about achieving your big goal. Go through your list of steps carefully and make sure that you have filled in all of the answers that will impact your mindset, preparation, and upcoming changes. Now we will look at the different types of investments you'll be required to make in yourself to make the brainstorming and relationship decisions pay off.

CHAPTER 7

Investments

"Stats Don't Lie"

Let's say you want to be one of the top golfers in the world, but you don't enjoy the same attributes as other elite golfers, like height, eye-hand coordination, or physical strength. This was what British-born Matt Fitzpatrick grappled with as a promising golf amateur when he reached his full height of 5' 9". He recognized his physical limitations would require a strategy that was tailored to his own situation, and that it would be foolish to just copy another golfer's training approach. Years later he reflected on the fateful course he set for himself at that time: "Some people are born with speed. I had to build mine."

And that he did. Fitzpatrick maximized every inch of his physical and psychological fortitude by working with a putting coach, a swing coach, a nutritionist, a mental strategist, a trainer, and a performance coach. He also chose to zero in on his self-described "data weirdo" tendencies as the key edge he could have over his competitors. Starting as a teen and to this day, Fitzpatrick logs every single practice and tournament shot he takes along with data about the club used, the lie of the hole, and as many as 20 other golf variables. The data is fed into a special computer program and he finetunes his practice based on what the data indicates. This can include focusing on specific challenges – like hitting the ball in varied weather conditions and from different angles on the same hole – which helps him to adapt more easily in disparate tournament conditions.

"He'll turn over every last stone to find that 1%," coach Mike Walker says admiringly. "And then he'll go out and find another stone." Fitzpatrick agrees: "Stats don't lie."

Although Fitzpatrick hasn't physically grown in stature in recent years, his golf prominence soared as a result of the regimented, data-driven lifestyle he designed to help him reach his goals. By the age of 29 he was ranked sixth in the world and was one of the pro golfers featured in the popular Netflix reality series *Full Swing*. When reporters asked what he thought other professionals could learn from his disciplined improvement, his criticism was blunt. "[They stand] in the same spot on the range and just [hit] at the same target over and over and over again. But I'm fine with them doing that – good for me."

One of the oft-repeated "zombie" goal statements – like SMART – is the "10,000 Hour Rule," which has been popularized in books and the media as the amount of time necessary to become elite in performing an action. Although the number is "sticky" and easy to remember, the truth is that the variable that matters is not the number of hours spent accumulating skills, it's the "deliberate practice" during that time that matters. Deliberate practice means spending time refining an action or thought, and rigorously measuring how much better or worse you are getting during those hours. This is similar to Matt Fitzpatrick practicing golf shots from different angles in different weather, and why he disdains the golfers who hit the same balls from the same spot over and over.

Big Goals Require Big Investments

The "I" in the BRIDGE methodology represents investments, and this is the step that truly separates the dreamers from the doers. We can fantasize about our big goals all day, create brilliant strategies to pursue those dreams, and then recruit an amazing team of cheerleaders and mentors who stand ready to teach us, coach us, support us, and believe in us, but none of these actions will matter unless you are willing, ready, and able to make the investments in yourself that will spell the difference between crossing a finish line and being an almost-ran. And the most important investment you'll need to make if you want to be successful is to spend your time wisely and well.

According to the 2022 American Time Use Survey, which measures the time people spend doing various activities, men and women have between 35 and 40 hours of leisure time every week (men average 5.6 hours a day and women average 4.8 hours a day), but these hours are often poorly spent. In fact, the survey showed that approximately 2.8 hours a day are spent watching television or some form of entertainment on a screen, which creates brainwaves akin to depression brainwaves. It's also been found that when a viewer binge watches a season of shows all at once, they wind up deenergized, unmotivated to take action, and emotionally empty. Why? It's thought that mindlessly watching others do things on screen for hours instead of taking action might deplete one's willpower, ambition, and energy.

All I Wanna Do Is Have Some Fun

Texas A&M football quarterback Johnny Manziel, who was the first player to win the Heisman Trophy as a college freshman, torpedoed any chance he had of succeeding in the National Football League because he refused to invest his time in watching game films or studying playbooks. He expected easy success and did not want to put effort toward learning how to comport himself as a paid professional.

Moving up to the big leagues was a learning goal for Manziel, not a performance goal. It wasn't about showing up hungover and playing ball with the same group of guys any longer. He was expected to adopt new behaviors, be open to learning more advanced football systems, harmoniously interact with a different set of teammates and coaches, and have the maturity to budget his time wisely.

But he wouldn't. His self-absorption, disregard for well-meaning advice from coaches, and poor play ultimately destroyed his career. It also didn't help that he surrounded himself in his free time with hangers-on and enablers of his worst instincts. Manziel's NFL contract was terminated after one year for immature behavior and sub-par performance, and he was completely out of football soon after.

What Are You Willing to Invest in Your Dream?

Fitzpatrick is a perfect example of someone who recognized that his big goal wouldn't and couldn't happen unless he committed time, money, and energy to honing his skills and knowledge with focus and discipline. Manziel was the opposite. Fitzpatrick's family was also willing to make sacrifices to support his dream because they witnessed his passion and willingness to follow through on doing the hard work required of him. Although Fitzpatrick's story may feel unrelatable to you because of his lofty stature in the golf world, reading about what he did to set himself up for the success he dreamed about might spur your thinking about the investments you will need to make in yourself to accomplish your own goals.

> "When you analyze happiness, it turns out that the way you spend your time is extremely important."
>
> *Daniel Kahneman*

"Yes" to This Means "No" to That

For example, one investment you might need to make is finding childcare providers and other helpers who will give you the flexibility to join a sports league, participate in a community play, or just have precious time to spend with family and friends. You may need to learn how to make a budget and shift your spending so that you can return to school or hire a career coach to guide you on how to change professions or advance in the one you are in. Your energy is finite, so if you want to volunteer for a political campaign or work on a social change movement, where will that time come from? What will you need to turn down to make that new investment of time and energy? These are typical of the decisions clients of mine have made to live their best lives without regret.

There are clever ways of making key investments if you are short on resources. For example, when money is tight, I've seen people arrange barters to exchange one of their skills for the knowledge of another person. I know an interior decorator who gave free renovation advice to a homeowner who agreed to train and board her dog while she traveled to visit her "bucket list" sights. There are also many "hacks" on TikTok and other social media that can help you save valuable time and money pursuing goals like building an outdoor shed to be a writer's cabin or setting up a soundproof studio to record a podcast or music.

- ♦ Will you need to invest money in a person or service to take tasks off your hands so that you can focus on what only you can do in your goal pursuit such as a virtual assistant, travel agent, dog walker? Where will you find them?
- ♦ Will you need to take a course online – free or paid – to improve your skills?
- ♦ Will you need to spend time getting to know someone who is new to you who will be an important part of your journey?

Forward-thinking financial planners are increasingly turning to Positive Psychology for tools to help clients expand their social capital – positive relationships – and not just their financial capital. If the goal is to create a flourishing life, every expert agrees that cultivating and maintaining close friendships pays incalculable dividends that can trump what's in the bank or 401(k). Not only do these relationships improve our well-being – an ingredient that fuels goal success – but they make us better people, too. Expect to invest 40–60 hours of one-on-one time with a new person to get a relationship off the ground, and be prepared to spend time in supporting them, celebrating with them, and sharing activities if you want to have that investment pay off in happiness, optimism, and a flourishing social circle.

Saving Trees, One Vine at a Time

After you list the investments that will be personally required of you and where you will find them, think creatively about where else you might find organizations, companies, or communities that might want to invest in you and your dream. For example, you might have access to resources in your company that you won't know about until you ask. It's not uncommon for corporations and communities to make specific resources and knowledge available to help their employees and citizens thrive and achieve important goals that elevate the quality of everyone around them. Finding out what is available to you and taking advantage of those assets might require some digging, but be thorough in your search because it can make the difference between success and near-success.

For example, a colleague of mine told me that his daughter had spent months looking for financial aid that would benefit women from her background with shared interests. Her research gave her the ability to cobble several scholarships together that made attending graduate school a reality. One of my neighbors is a lawyer who loves being outside in nature, and when he saw a sign at the local library about how the county trains volunteers to identify and cut down invasive vines, he signed up and it gave his life renewed meaning. Whenever he is walking his dog or has free time, he can be found with a knife in the neighborhood woods saving trees and other shrubs from the vines that are choking and killing them.

A survey of women who rose to the top of their profession and what they did to achieve their goals found an important common denominator: they outsourced as many tasks as possible that took them away from being the best person and working professional they could be. In a practical sense this meant that they invested in – or bartered with – live-in *au pairs*, clothes shoppers, house cleaners, and other sources of help that allowed them to use their time in ways that made them feel like they were becoming their "ideal selves."

Investing in Others' Dreams

Some companies offer a paid month's leave to employees after a certain number of years, which is designed to free them up to pursue a calling or further a personal dream. Best Buy's former CEO, Hubert Joly, started his turnaround of the company in 2012 when it was on death's doorstep, and one of the strategies he used to build a motivated, engaged workforce was to ask them what their dreams were, and how working at Best Buy could help them to achieve their goals. "We invest in people," he explained. "It creates magic."

I saw this philosophy come to life several years ago when I spoke about goal setting and grit at a gathering of 1,000 lululemon managers. A store manager – "Lola" – approached me afterward to share her own story of goals and grit, and the role the company had played in an important personal achievement. A year before my visit, Lola's supervisor had asked her to identify her biggest dream. She replied that she longed to compete in the Kona Ironman event, but that the entry fee was so high that she had temporarily shelved the goal.

A few months later Lola was standing at the company's awards banquet when a giant screen lit up behind her with a note telling her that the company had paid her entrance fee and the costs of the plane fare to and from the race. Her face aglow as she related her story, Lola asked me to consider telling her story in future speeches because of the lesson she had learned from her good fortune.

"What if I had never told anyone my dream?" she asked me, eyes wide. "Make sure people know that telling your dream to the right people can help make it come true!"

- ◆ Who are the "right people" who know about your big goal and who might want to invest in you with their time, energy, money, and/or goodwill?
- ◆ Are you investing in other people to help them achieve their big goals? Robert Cialdini, author of the bestseller *Influence*, says being reciprocal – doing something for someone because that person has done something for you – is so powerful that every human society practices this behavior.

People Want to Be Part of Your Dream

Nowhere was this more evident than in the feel-good story of Mexican athlete German Madrazo, who had always had a dream of being an Olympian, but his efforts at becoming elite in his chosen sports had never gotten him far enough. Unwilling to give up his lofty (some might even say "unrealistic"!) goal, he decided to try to qualify for the 2018 Winter Olympics in the punishing cold weather sport of cross-country skiing. Although many people scoffed at the outlandish dream of representing Mexico in a sport that required snow, others believed in him and invested their time in coaching him, housing him as he traveled around Europe accumulating competition points, and encouraging him whenever he got discouraged.

Madrazo did ultimately qualify, and his passion for making his dream come true was one of the most-reported feel-good stories of the 2018 Olympics. When he initially carried his country's flag into the Olympic stadium along with three other Mexican athletes at the start of the Games, he received thunderous applause. And although Madrazo finished dead last in his punishing 10,000 km cross-country skiing event – 30 minutes behind the winner – the other competitors were waiting for him with the Mexican flag when he finished, hoisting him on their shoulders in celebration.

One year later, when I interviewed Madrazo about the reception the other athletes had given him despite his last place finish, he paused and his voice caught in his throat. "Caroline, I learned that when your dream is big enough, people catch your passion, and they want to be part of it. It was the biggest lesson and greatest experience of my entire life."

Would You Wear That to Your Grandmother's House?

Sometimes a company must invest in their employees because it has no choice, and those investments might be a welcome surprise that can spur you forward with your big goals. The media is filled with stories about the different ways this is happening, and I have my own personal story to share about what I witnessed as a mother in this respect.

When my oldest son, Haywood, joined KPMG, a big four accounting firm, after graduating from college, he had to learn several things that others might take for granted in the workplace. As a Division I swimmer who had been clothed in sweatsuits or sponsored athletic gear for years, and who had done one or two workouts every day since the age of 8, he had almost no idea what to wear in an office, at casual work settings, or when meeting clients in person. It turns out he wasn't alone. For years, KPMG has routinely gathered their young associates at conferences for fashion shows that instruct them on proper clothing etiquette. "If you wouldn't wear it to visit your grandmother, it's not a good idea to wear it to meet with clients," they insist.

Hello! My Name Is . . .

The Millennial and Gen Z generations that grew up with screens in their hands, and who lost several years of in-person interactions and educational instruction, have shown up in the workplace with more deficits than not knowing what to wear. Media reports are that young adults now must be tutored in how to write professional emails that don't open with "Hey!" or that don't feature emojis and acronyms like CYA or LOL; one major investment bank even sent guidelines about how to avoid drinking to excess at gatherings with clients. Companies are also investing in consultants and coaches who give workshops on how to make presentations, work cooperatively in groups, and hold conversations with superiors that don't use filler words like "um" in every sentence. Michigan State University Business School goes one step further to help young graduates build friendships. They instruct students to introduce themselves by their first and last name, and then: "STOP! Let them tell you their name," they counsel.

A retired Princeton chemistry professor who authored an acclaimed textbook in the field was so passionate about his topic that he offered to teach the course at a reduced rate at a state university on an annual contract. He was shocked by the students' unwillingness to invest the hours the course required, and how

(continued)

surprised the students were when they received failing grades. To help, he offered many after-hours prep classes and had an open-door policy of assisting any students who needed extra support. The students' exam results barely changed, however, and instead of putting time toward learning better ways to study and achieve the marks they needed to pass and go to graduate school, the students put together a petition to have the professor removed because his class was "too hard." He was fired.

♦ Be smart about taking advantage of the efforts others make on your behalf to do things like learn how to study more effectively, budget your time and money wisely, and add skills on the job to become more marketable. Have you investigated opportunities to assist you that are being provided by your school, your coach, your company, or your community?

What Is Your Time Worth?

Greg McDonough is an entrepreneur who juggles running his consulting business with training for Ironman competitions and being an active father to two teen daughters with his wife, Monique. Greg has an unerring knack for knowing what his "genius work" is and what he should outsource to achieve his goals with the excellence he expects of himself. In the many years I have worked with him as his coach, he has invested in the products and people that he knows matter most to guarding his time for the areas that are most important to him.

For example, he opted to invest in a fledgling service to take his racing bicycle from his home to an Ironman competition after an airline banged it up, rendering it almost unusable once he arrived at the race. Instead of wasting time on do-it-yourself podcasting, he hired an organization to record and produce his "Endurance Leadership" shows, saving him valuable hours that are better spent elsewhere.

To make these investments, Greg created a time and money budget for the year, decided how to marry the time and money allotments with his available resources, and then put other ideas and businesses he was interested in pursuing into a "parking lot" for future attention. By using this type of thoughtful care around how and where his time would go in the coming year, a review of where he was six months later revealed that he had made more consistently excellent progress in those six months than in the years when he hadn't been as thoughtful.

> The average American has four to six hours of leisure time every day (women average an hour less than men) but that time is often spent in front of television and other screens, not pursuing hobbies or learning.

Here are some points to ponder as you begin to list the investments you will need to make for your big goal:

- If you have a learning goal of doing your first running race or becoming comfortable speaking Japanese so that you can do a semester abroad, you may not have any sense of the size of the investments you might need to make. In a world of scams and clickbait, rely on trusted websites and people to give you the knowledge you need to fill out your investment budget list. Be thorough in your research so that your calculations won't cause you pain down the road as the result of buying an untested product or using an overpriced service.
- For those with a performance goal who already have an accurate sense of the range of investments you will need to make in your success, your task is to get updated information about which resources you habitually rely on that have been improved, or if a competitor now offers a better approach. For example, when I am writing a book, I know I must invest in long periods of time when I am alone in a co-working space or an isolated cabin in the woods. Because I've written so many books on deadline, I have a checklist I consult to gauge if costs have changed on things like printer ink, and I assess my available writing hours compared to immovable events on my calendar (like two children's weddings while

writing this book!). Once I have that information, I am pretty accurate about what I can and can't do, and what the size and type of investments I need to make look like compared to previous books.

> Even though writing books is a performance goal for me, I always go into deadline-specific goals with questions like, "Is there anything that will make me healthier and more productive during my writing periods?" In this case, because I signed the contract during the winter and I had a business trip to Malaysia that would strain my physical capacity between two of the publisher's deadlines, I invested in bi-weekly therapeutic I.V. treatments for three months to replenish any lost fluids and keep my energy up, which definitely allowed me to work longer, smarter hours and stay healthy under pressure. Performance goals will always benefit from small tweaks like this, and the prompts to identify what you can do better on your performance goals should revolve around the availability of newer, better ways to get to the same excellent outcome.

Doing the Basics

Once you become aware of the activities and exercises that will be part of your goal pursuit – either ones that you know work for you, or ones that are new to you – think about how much time you'll need to invest in those processes. Will it be daily? Weekly? How will you know? Here is a sample of some of the basic activities that are often investments of time and effort for people who are focused on accomplishing big goals:

- ◆ **Building habits with improved willpower.** Once the goal is clear, identify the self-regulation behaviors that will accelerate your progress and boost your commitment and follow-through. One of my clients set a goal of enlarging his base of financial management clients and he made himself accountable for one hour of outreach calls every Monday and Friday morning, which his assistant helped with by screening his calls and not scheduling any client meetings.

◆ **Amplifying well-being with daily positive interventions.**
Since the research is clear that well-being is a necessary ingredient for the mindset and behavior that maximizes chances of goal success, everyone should know and practice the activities, thoughts, interactions, and behaviors that boost their flourishing. Since people are different and don't all respond to interventions in the same way, clarify what works for you by experimenting with different actions. Many people use morning physical exercise to get them going and improve optimism and energy, some use journal writing or spiritual reflection to center themselves and practice gratitude, and some make sure to connect with loved ones to hear laughter or express their appreciation.

Time Waits for No One

I keep returning to the importance of judging the time you'll need to invest in the pursuit of your goal because this is where I see people making the biggest mistakes. Either they underestimate the number of hours it will take to learn something new or they fail to budget the time they will need to explore all of the "what if?" considerations that need to be included in a goal timeline. Give yourself sufficient space to puzzle through the investments questions included here, and talk to other people who have knowledge of how much time they or others had to take to make a big change in their behavior, or in accomplishing a key step that led them closer to success.

◆ **Will you need to set aside days, weeks, months, or years to add the skills or knowledge you require to succeed?**
Base your answers on as much solid knowledge as possible by interviewing people who have done what you want to do and who are like you in terms of how they incorporate new information into their lives. For example, if you want to learn a martial art so that you can have usable self-defense skills, watch classes at several studios first, meet the instructors you would be working with, look at the schedule of class times to see if they match your availability, and interview someone who has the martial arts skills that you want. If you have dyslexia, ADHD, or another condition that requires that you optimize learning in a certain way, factor that into your

scrutiny of different programs. I've seen too many clients and acquaintances assume that virtual learning would work for them because it worked for a friend, only to discover a month into the class that it wasn't effective, and they couldn't reclaim their investment of time and money.

◆ **Will you need to invest time and money in therapy or another positive avenue to conquer a disabling fear (fear of flying, for example) or put your past into a different perspective (work on forgiveness to move away from time-consuming rumination, for example)?** Choosing someone to partner with to help you prepare for an important mental shift is like choosing a spouse or investment partner. Don't just go into the same therapy or coaching program that a friend or colleague is using. Be choosy as you research and interview different people to make sure that you are matching your needs with the resource that is most likely to benefit you. The time you invest in these types of actions will prevent you from circling back later if a hasty decision sets you back.

◆ Go through the answers you've given to the questions in this chapter and summarize the amounts of time, energy, and other resources you'll require to maximize your chances of success. Include the investments you've located that are available to you either free or at cost. Add the investments you've discovered that other people have made available to people like you in your organization, community, or elsewhere. Put all of this together and include these answers in your master strategy list.

Halfway Across Your Bridge to the Future

Now that you have identified an important goal and used the right kind of brainstorming to think around curves, anticipate curveballs, given attention to the people you need to include (and avoid), and clearly listed the many large and small investments that are necessary to have a solid blueprint for action, you are ready for instruction on how you can shape your decision-making skills to avoid bias, build on previous positive actions, and know when to pivot in a better direction.

CHAPTER 8

Decision-Making

What Were You Thinking?

You can trace some of the twenty-first century's saddest black swan events to a fateful decision that was made by one man, based on misplaced values, that was taken for the wrong reasons.

It was the spring of 2011, and the president of American Airlines, Gerard Arpey, called W. James McNerney, Jr., Boeing's leader, with bad news. "We're going to place a big order with Airbus for their new long-haul, fuel-efficient planes," he said. "Why haven't you guys kept up with their innovation and scrappiness?"

Boeing had always relied on American to help keep its profits fat and its stock high, not to mention ensure fat pay packages for McNerney and Boeing's other senior executives. American's defection would be a disaster.

McNerney begged Arpey to hold off. He promised that Boeing would renovate its popular 737 model within 6 years (the 737 Max rolled off the assembly line in 4), instead of investing the 10 years that is common when designing a new plane. The plan would save Boeing money and would be an easier, cheaper way to keep American and other airlines as happy customers who would stay in the Boeing fold.

The decision to retrofit the old 737 plane instead of carefully designing a safe upgrade sent Boeing's employees into "hectic" overdrive, pushing engineers to double their normal pace of producing technical drawings in what was described as "an intense pressure cooker."

The engineers were ordered to avoid designing anything that would lead to a requirement for pilots to train in a simulator, which would drive up Boeing's costs and prevent the plane from getting into service.

Boeing had to match Airbus's fuel-efficient engines that made the longer flights possible, however, so the designs featured bigger engines, changing the plane's aerodynamics. The result was the addition of software, called MCAS, which would control many of the plane's actions if it sensed changes in the nose direction or a trajectory shift, triggering multiple sirens and warning lights going off at once. Pilots were never informed of these design changes or allowed to train on how to respond to the terrifying alarm bells that resulted, or what to do when a faulty sensor sent the plane nose-down-outcomes that were inextricably linked to McNerney's decision to push a new plane into the world too quickly by cutting corners to keep the cash coming.

In October 2018 and March 2019, two 737 Max planes crashed shortly after takeoff, killing everyone on board – 346 men, women, and children. Boeing was ordered to ground hundreds of planes for almost two years to undergo safety checks and train pilots, but the company is still reeling from the MCAS malfunctions and other safety mishaps that dog the company on a near-daily basis.

Whistleblowers continue to come forward with jarring reports of a culture of rule-breaking, lax safety standards, and intolerance for anyone who stands up to corporate malfeasance (and two of them died within two months of each other in early 2024). It seems that every week another Boeing plane experiences a scary episode, from a door being sucked out of an Alaska Airlines flight midway through a January 2024 trip, to sensors, engines, and safety slides being inoperable with no warning. Boeing, once one of the most trustworthy corporations in the country, is in a downward spiral of bleeding cash and lost credibility, and doubters wonder if it will avoid bankruptcy or ever reclaim its sterling reputation.

To achieve big goals, you will need to know how to make your best decisions – the "D" in the BRIDGE approach – about when to act, when you need to pause your plans, when you should change course, and when to take a risk – although you may not have enough information to guarantee success. Great leaders learn how to create a track record of trusting themselves and the team around them to make big decisions and keep going, and the story of one of them follows.

"I Believe You Can Find a Way"

Susan Tynan couldn't believe it. She had vacationed in several US National Parks with her sister and returned with four cheap posters she wanted to get framed. When she took them to a framing store, though, she was informed that the price would be $1,600. No other options existed so she agreed to the price, but the sticker shock and inability to find reasonable alternatives stuck with her. Tynan was certain that if she was appalled by the exorbitant prices, other people must be, too. She thought there had to be a better way, so she set out to find it.

Up until that moment, Tynan had never been an entrepreneur, but her father had been the president of a tugboat company, and she had grown up seeing how much work was involved in being the head of an organization with multiple responsibilities. She knew from listening to his stories that investing in others was necessary if you wanted to succeed in any endeavor.

Tynan's education at Harvard Business School had reinforced those early lessons; the homework revolved around case studies of leaders who had overcome adversity to accomplish big goals, as well as those whose decisions had brought down their organizations. Disrupting the entrenched mom-and-pop framing industry was going to require knowledge Tynan lacked and the support of skilled people she could trust to make good decisions. Undeterred by the enormity of her goal, she took the plunge to learn about the industry and found the right people to help her succeed.

After careful research – even taking a framing course to understand how it was done – Tynan launched Framebridge in 2014, a custom online framing business that later expanded into brick-and-mortar stores. She broke records for raising more venture funding than any other woman-founded company in the Washington, D.C. area, and was among the top 25 women-led businesses in the country that received venture support (most are technology-focused, making the financial backing she received even more exceptional). She was named CEO of the Year by *Washington Business Journal* in

2019, among many other honors since the company's inception, and in 2022 Harvard Business School published a case study on Tynan's company: "Framebridge: Reimagining Custom Framing."

Although Tynan's story looks like a seamless journey from good idea to successful disruption of an established field, she has had to take countless risks that were not for the faint-hearted. Some of them paid off, and some didn't. To guide her, she relied on a set of values that helped her to choose what to do at times.

She elaborated in an interview: "I'm never going to be unethical, and I'm never gonna be negligent. So I can take investor money. I can try this. And if I fail, so be it. One of the most wonderful things about the United States is if you fail as an entrepreneur, you're not permanently penalized for it." She also believes in betting on herself and teaching others to do the same when making important decisions. Her mantra: "I believe you can find a way."

The word "decide" derives from two Latin words: *decider* (to kill) and *caedere* (to cut). When people are deciding to do things, they are "cutting off" alternatives, and some poetically say that deciding is "killing off" ideas in order to come to a conclusion.

A Bias for Action

Tynan's approach to risk-taking is instructive for anyone who will need to choose when to move forward with a goal, when to stop pursuing a course of action because it is not working, and when to jump on an opportunity and suddenly act because a promising lead has presented itself.

First, she educates herself about whether the potential upside of taking action will match one of the company's values, like "bias for action" or "build to last." She also loves to go through daily metrics to inform her thinking, like store foot traffic, marketing initiatives, and speed of framing turnaround during year-end holiday sales, which is when Framebridge does the bulk of its business.

Tynan laser focuses on the data that translates directly to creating sales and satisfied customers and is quick to make changes if the data tell her a story that won't help Framebridge achieve its goals.

She also leans heavily on the input of the team she has assembled, which is a sophisticated mix of people who specialize in design, manufacturing, marketing, customer service, and retail. Tynan is acutely aware of what her unique strengths are and she understands that others in her senior leadership team know better than she does about how to run an efficient factory, or how to create financial scenario analyses, and she has the humility to trust them and give them the authority to do what's best.

Learning and Performance Goals Pursued Simultaneously

Framebridge has been a long series of learning goals for Tynan – for example, learning how to raise venture money, learning how to be a CEO, learning how to lead a company through a pandemic and keep the brick-and-mortar stores thriving, learning what customers want most in an online framing business, learning how to hire and fire people, and much more – but she also has performance goals that help her set annual sales goals and have the confidence that they will be achieved. Now that she has several factories run by experienced leaders who have trained their employees in how to frame with the company's exacting standards, she can predict with accuracy how many orders can be accepted and turned around within a guaranteed timeframe at different times of the year, while still getting high marks from satisfied customers.

Lessons from Starbucks to Taylor Swift

To continue to evolve as the best leader she can be, Tynan regularly meets with and learns from other CEOs who have impressive records as business leaders and who have "brought joy to their customers." She cites people like Howard Schulz, founder of Starbucks, and Danny Meyer, the restaurateur who runs Shake Shack, for their attention to detail and for making the customer feel valued and seen.

The business leader who inspires her the most, though, is singer Taylor Swift, whose talent, chutzpah, attention to her fans, and demonstrated business acumen have made her one of the most influential and successful figures – male or female – of the twenty-first century. Tynan and her two daughters are devoted "Swifties" who dress in costume and attend concerts to dance and sing along with Swift, whose extraordinary performances awe Tynan and concert crowds with their length and superior choreography. Given her passion for artistry, excellence, and pleasing the customer, it's no surprise to learn that Tynan harbors the big goal that one day Swift will mention Framebridge in one of her songs. Given Tynan's track record for getting things done, I'm betting on it.

- ◆ Think about risks you've taken and what results you got from those risks. Were your risks well-reasoned? Is there anything you would do to change your approach as you map out an action plan of decision-making for your goal success?

The "Human Computer" and the Astronaut

John Glenn was about to become the first American to orbit Earth when he made a request prior to going into quarantine in December, 1961 to prepare for the Friendship 7 launch. "Get the girl to check the numbers."

Glenn was referring not to a "girl," but to the 44-year-old math genius Katherine Johnson, who was known at NASA's Flight Research Division at the Langley Research Center in Hampton, Virginia as a "human computer." It had been her work of calculating by hand the orbital trajectories that had gotten astronaut Alan Shepard safely into space and back home in May 1961 as the first American to make that trip, and now Glenn wanted her to double-check the numbers for his own trajectory. Computers were relatively new at the time, and were known to make errors, so Glenn's decision to launch himself into orbit relied on Johnson fact-checking the computer's equations. Only after she spent several days going through the numbers and giving her okay did Glenn agree to fly his mission.

- When have you made your best decisions about taking action to do something important? Write down as many variables as possible that have mattered in your stories of good decision-making. What was the time of day? Where were you? Were you alone or with certain people?
- Is there anyone you trust who has always given you good advice when you needed it?
- Whose decision-making do you admire and why?

Is Your Decision Biased?

Daniel Kahneman, the Nobel Prize winning psychologist and economist, published *Thinking Fast and Slow* in 2011 about the hidden sources of bias, leading many organizations to create workshops and trainings on how to avoid bias when hiring, promoting, and giving feedback, among many other decisions that can influence the fate and success of others. In recent years, Diversity, Equity, and Inclusion (DEI) programs were launched to educate employees on the ways that our biases lead us to discriminate against others by making and acting on faulty assumptions that we might not be aware of.

Here are some examples of the most commonly cited biases:

- **Confirmation Bias:** This occurs when a person favors information that confirms their preexisting beliefs. For example, an investor might focus only on news that suggests a positive outlook for a stock they own, ignoring any negative indicators.
- **Anchoring Bias:** This is the tendency to rely too heavily on the first piece of information received when making decisions. For instance, if the first house a buyer sees is listed at $500,000, they might judge all subsequent houses based on this initial price.
- **Stereotyping:** Making assumptions about individuals based on their membership in a group, rather than on their own merits. For example, a hiring manager might assume a candidate will not fit the team culture based on their ethnicity or gender.
- **Survivorship Bias:** This bias occurs when only successful entities are considered, ignoring the failures. An example is when

companies analyze only their successful products to develop new ones, without considering why other products failed.

♦ **Optimism Bias:** The tendency to think that we are less at risk of experiencing a negative event compared to others. For example, a person might believe they are less likely to get sick and therefore neglect necessary health precautions.

How Biased Are You?

Examine the above list of biases and think about times when bias interfered with good judgment, and as a result, you did not make a decision that was in your best interests or the interests of others. For example:

♦ Did you choose a partner for a group project because you think people from that culture are naturally smarter and harder-working?

♦ Did you greenlight a project at work because you believed a previous success meant it couldn't fail, and you didn't examine if another approach would work in a similar situation but with different variables?

♦ Did you decide that the person who spoke the most in a team meeting was more competent and knowledgeable about the topic being discussed because others didn't speak up? How did this judgment (or a similar one) impact current or future outcomes?

Where There Is Judgment, There Is Noise

Kahneman followed up his influential book on bias with *Noise: A Flaw in Human Judgment* in 2016 (co-authored with Olivier Sibony and Cass Sunstein). The authors define "noise" in making judgments and decision-making as "undesirable variability in judgments of the same problem," adding, "[w]herever there is judgment, there is noise, and more of it than you think." Before Kahneman passed away in early 2024, he declared that noise was a more important factor in poor decision-making than bias because he and others concluded that it leads to injustice, unacceptable health hazards, and a loss of time and health, among other damaging outcomes.

Understanding the differences between noise and bias, and taking note of yourself in several scenarios where you are making a decision or taking an action, will help you make your best decisions in goal pursuit going forward. Not being able to separate the two and take corrective action when you spot their emergence can be as damaging to your goal success as not understanding the differences between learning goals and performance goals.

Here are some examples of noise in decision-making offered by Kahneman, Sibony, and Sunstein in their book:

- **Judgment Variability:** Different judges might sentence similar crimes with significantly different penalties based on their personal interpretations and mood, rather than based on a consistent application of the law.
- **Medical Diagnosis:** Two doctors might give different diagnoses or treatment recommendations for the same medical condition based on subjective judgment influenced by factors such as fatigue or differing levels of experience.
- **Financial Estimation:** Loan officers at a bank may provide different interest rates or loan amounts to identical loan applications simply because they interpret the bank's lending criteria differently or assess risk differently.
- **Human Resources:** Different HR personnel might interpret the qualifications and potential of a job candidate differently, leading to variance in whom they consider the best candidate for a position.
- **Quality Control:** In manufacturing, inspectors might have varying assessments of what constitutes a defect, leading to inconsistent product quality leaving the factory floor.

Is It Bias or Is It Noise?

Here are specific real-world examples to help you further clarify the differences between noise and bias and how they can creep into your day-to-day thinking and decision-making:

- Imagine your bathroom scale always shows that you're four pounds lighter; that's bias. If the number varies each time you step on the scale, despite your weight being constant, then it's noisy.

- Say you are a lawyer, and you are representing a client who is seeking parole. Equally qualified judges might give you completely different verdicts depending on whether or not it is the end of the workday (decision fatigue) or if their favorite sports team lost a big game the previous day. This is noise.

- Think about Olympic figure skating and diving judges who give different scores on the same athletic trick, depending on jet lag and hunger cues being altered because of travel. That's noise. If they routinely score athletes from their own countries higher than athletes from different countries – regardless of the time of day or length of time in the host country – that is bias.

- Some pathologists reading x-rays have been found to vary widely in their opinions on different days, and a human resources person might hire one person on a day when they slept well but turn down an identical candidate a week later if they are not rested. Again, this is noise, and the randomness can lead to deviations that cost companies billions of dollars.

- A referee in an American football game might give a player a "roughing the passer" penalty in a championship game where stakes are high but overlook that same penalty a week later in another championship game, potentially leading to a loss that could cost a head coach their job or result in a player trade that upends and harms a family's health, emotional stability, and earning power. Making a different judgment in the same situation is noise.

While noise and bias look similar in many examples, the more you study them, the easier it is to discern what makes bias different from noise, and why these decision-making errors can wreak so much havoc in one's personal and professional lives.

- Do a "noise audit" on your decisions for one week. Compare decisions you've made about the same topic on different days to discover your own inconsistencies.

♦ Make a checklist of your desired decision-making steps for some of the situations that you think or know will emerge while pursuing your goal. This could include how you will make decisions when you are tired, how you will evaluate the factors involved in risk-taking when you are around certain people, and what you will do to check yourself if you feel you are tending toward making a noisy decision.

Computer-generated algorithms have been compared to human decision-making where noise is likely, and it has found that algorithms are so bias-free and factual in their answers that they trump decision-making in most settings. While algorithms can offer a noise-free solution by consistently applying the same rules to the same inputs, they aren't always feasible or accepted in every context. In cases where professional judgment must remain, fostering consistency involves training, structured decision-making processes, and tools like checklists to guide judgments. Noise is what Atul Gawande was combatting when he introduced checklists into surgery. Kahneman agreed, noting that checklists would help to prevent overconfidence in decision-making, which is what is often spotted in highly trained professionals who don't think noise enters their decision-making.

How Texas Hold 'Em Teaches Decision-Making

Jenny Just's husband was disgusted when he watched their 14-year-old daughter lose her tennis match against her opponent because he didn't think she was playing to win or trying to anticipate her opponent's moves. He came home and vented to his wife, a billionaire from her successful financial services company. "She needs to learn how to play poker!"

Just has now formed Poker Power, which is on a mission to teach women and girls to play poker because of the ways it can translate into helping them learn how to take more risks, something that men are more likely to do, especially in high stakes situations. She has found that when she is hiring women to work at her investment firm,

Peak6, they lack the confidence to make decisions about when to invest in the options market unless they have all the relevant information in front of them, which she says can hold them back in her business. She encourages learning poker because the options market and poker are identical: they both involve imperfect amounts of information, but you bet on a probable outcome and then change your strategy as more information comes in.

Two other women have become famous for their forays into Texas Hold 'Em poker. Annie Duke, author of *Thinking in Bets* and *Quit: The Power of Knowing When to Walk Away*, is the first woman to win the World Series of Poker Tournament of Champions, and she won more than $4 million in competitive poker tournaments all over the world. Maria Konnikova turned her career as a Harvard-educated psychologist who was fascinated by John von Neumann's "game theory" into a study of poker to explore its interplay of skill and chance. Her book about this endeavor, *The Biggest Bluff*, became a *New York Times* bestseller in 2020. In it she described how she used her psychology training to win against tables full of men (fewer than 5% of competitive poker players are women) who were unaware of their bias toward women, and who paid mightily for their blind spot when her bluffs worked.

To craft the strategy that helped her win in this male-dominated and macho environment, Konnikova took notes after her encounters with men whenever they spoke, analyzing the words they used and how they treated her. For example, she found if she acted helpless or flirtatious while playing, the men often showed her their cards to "teach" her how to play. When she took their money and then dropped her act, she would cheekily remind them that there are "no friends at the poker table."

Only 20% of hands that win at the poker table are the best hands. That means that if you want to win in any situation, you need to know how to bluff, read people, and take calculated risks with imperfect information while acting like you have a winning hand. Estee Lauder, founder of the cosmetics company that still bears her name, was frustrated when major department stores wouldn't carry her lipstick when she launched her product, so she would go to luncheons and have women try it on (even putting it on them herself!). If they were satisfied and asked where to buy the product, she would tell them to go to one of the department stores that had turned her down. After numerous women went to those stores and asked where the Estee Lauder counter was, the stores believed she was a bigger success than she was, and her sales took off. Lauder later said, "No one ever became a success without taking chances . . . [O]ne must be able to recognize the moment and seize it without delay."

◆ Can you think of how bluffing effectively in some situations can help you achieve your goal? Many entrepreneurs tell stories about getting their biggest orders for a new product by pretending that they have already made big sales, or that they can do something they've never done before.

Poker Takeaways for Better Decisions

◆ **Think of Decisions as Bets:** Every decision you make is a bet on your future. Thinking of it this way sharpens your mind, making you consider the possibilities more critically and helping you choose smarter paths.

◆ **Focus on the Process, Not Just the Result:** Good choices can sometimes lead to unexpected results, similar to a perfect shot in basketball that inexplicably misses. Judge your decisions based on how well you made them, not just on what ends up happening.

◆ **Challenge Wishful Thinking:** It's tempting to believe something because it's what you want to happen. Always base your decisions on solid evidence, not just on hopes. This clear-sighted approach leads to more reliable outcomes.

◆ **Create a Diverse Decision-Making Team:** Surround yourself with a team that brings different perspectives to your decision-making process. This group should value honesty and open-mindedness, acting as your personal think tank to navigate complex choices.

♦ **Be Selective with Your Decisions:** Not every decision demands deep analysis. Learn to identify when to delve deeper and when to go with simpler, more straightforward choices. This strategy prevents decision fatigue and keeps you sharp for the big choices.

♦ **Seek Diverse Opinions:** Don't hesitate to seek out advice. Consulting with others can provide new insights and help you avoid blind spots. It's like having a cheat sheet that helps you ace the test of decision-making.

♦ **Manage Your Emotions:** In decision-making, staying calm and composed is crucial, much like maintaining composure under pressure in sports. If emotions run high, take a step back to clear your head, ensuring your decisions are rational and well-thought-out.

Can I Win This Hand with My Strategy?

Pull together and summarize the answers to the questions from earlier in this chapter, and then tweak those answers as if you are at a poker table attempting to win the hand so that you can stay in the game.

♦ Am I considering all possible "hands" before making a decision?
♦ Am I letting recent losses or wins affect my current decision-making?
♦ How am I managing my "risk" in this decision?
♦ When has noise gotten in the way of making good decisions, and when has bias had the same impact? Are either clouding my vision now?

Now it is time to turn our attention to the "X factor" known as grit, which is what we will need when we have done our homework and created big goals, examined the relevant relationships, listed the necessary investments, and taken stock of how to make our best decisions. While all of those factors matter, nothing gets us over a finish line better than knowing how to summon up courage, passion, persistence, and hope when we need it the most.

CHAPTER 9

Good Grit

The "X Factor" of Success

When I was a student at the University of Pennsylvania pursuing my Master's degree in Applied Positive Psychology, I frequently saw a cheerful woman with stacks of paper in her arms bustling in and out of our classrooms, usually to talk to Marty Seligman, who was supervising her PhD research on a quality she and Marty were calling "grit." While she was deepening her studies and creating a "Grit Scale" to measure a person's grit level, I was writing my Capstone on goals, which became my book *Creating Your Best Life*.

I wanted the book to be as comprehensive and evidence-based as possible, and since I was including Locke and Latham's work on the importance of "challenging and specific" goals for best performance, plus the finding that happy people wake up to hard goals that are outside their comfort zone, I decided to add a chapter about Angela Duckworth's tantalizing findings on the quality that was apparently behind the accomplishment of our hardest goals – grit. In fact, I was so intrigued by her work and the nerve she struck all over the world with the publication of her book, *Grit*, that I spent the next 10 years immersed in every aspect of what grit is and what it is not.

Beast Barracks and the National Spelling Bee

Duckworth defines grit as "passion and perseverance in pursuit of long-term goals," and her research has found that it predicts several successful outcomes in very hard goals, including remaining enrolled at West Point after surviving the hellish "Beast Barracks" summer during a plebe's first year, becoming a finalist at the National Spelling Bee, and making a special forces squad. Despite grit being challenged as "old wine in a new bottle" by academics who complained that it was just a restatement of the quality of conscientiousness or self-efficacy, she has replicated her findings to show that grit is, indeed, a quality that is distinct from discipline, conscientiousness, self-efficacy, follow-through, and resilience.

> Resilience is the ability to overcome short-term setbacks and adversity. Grit includes resilience, but it describes the mindset and behavior that it takes to pursue long-term goals with passion and a sense of purpose. You can be a resilient person and not have a specific goal, nor does displaying resilience imply that you bring passion to goal pursuit.

Duckworth has tweaked the Grit Scale test in recent years to better measure passion's role in displaying grit because she finds that it is the secret sauce that gives gritty people the ability to do hard things whether they are rewarded with public recognition, a trophy, extra compensation, or nothing. Gritty people pursue meaningful, hard goals that reflect their inner longings and dreams, and they do them to satisfy themselves and no one else. Many of the goals described in this book, like Dara Torres's attempt to win Olympic gold in swimming at the age of 41, are so hard that without the type of passion required to sustain grit, it would be far too easy to give up.

Ordinary Grit, Mt. Rushmore Grit, and Mt. Olympus Grit

My own view of grit from the perspective of an executive coach showed me that people who wanted to do very hard things often needed to upgrade their actions and mindset to improve their grit reserves, along with displaying other qualities like humility, emotional flourishing, and optimism that are also part of good grit.

I decided that my definition of "authentic grit" was slightly different from Duckworth's because I saw that the type of good grit that had the best impact in day-to-day life amplified its positive impact by uplifting the emotions and behaviors of others, as well.

As I studied these paragons of authentic grit, I found that they fell into different categories. They included "ordinary grit" (those you encounter in everyday life who are overcoming adversity without whining), "Mt. Olympus grit" (people who push their bodies to redefine what is possible), "celebrity grit" (famous people like Oprah who accomplished hard things against all odds and used their platform to make a difference), and "Mt. Rushmore grit" (people who impacted history by working to stand up against ingrained social wrongs with dignity and self-respect, like Gandhi and Martin Luther King).

I saw how they awed and inspired other people to challenge themselves to dig a little deeper to see what they could accomplish if they pursued their own big goals with grit. I now believe that grit is best when it doesn't just help us do hard things, but it also makes other people better because they witnessed or read about how and why grit was an important ingredient in that success.

> Authentic grit, as I define it, is the passionate pursuit of hard goals outside your comfort zone that awe and inspire others to ask themselves, "What if I had the courage to pursue my dreams and live life without regrets?" This type of good grit embraces risk-taking to accomplish one's own big goals, attracts the right people into your life, and unleashes positive energy; bad grit repels and diminishes you, and it has the capacity to destroy any chance of goal success by harming yourself or others.

I also wrote in my book *Getting Grit* (2017) that I believed anyone who wanted to cultivate good grit could do so, and that it would always start with setting a big goal. Locke and Latham identified the importance of "commitment" to one's goals to achieve "challenging and specific" outcomes, and Bandura's self-efficacy theory showed how believing that one had the ability to achieve the goal could lay the groundwork for acting resilient or gritty. But Locke, Latham, and Bandura did not anticipate the nuances that would later emerge when it came to accomplishing goals that were not simply "challenging and specific," but that were so extraordinary that a different term might need to emerge to explain goal accomplishment at different levels.

I believe grit can be cultivated at any age in the right conditions and with the right goal. My recovery from bulimia at a time when most people didn't believe you could overcome it is when I grew my own grit. It took a challenging and specific personal goal, commitment, a positive support system, an investment in learning new ways to eat and live, and the passion and persistence to keep going in the face of relapse and other setbacks, that changed my life and gave me the confidence that I could do other hard things. Growing grit was the most important turning point of my early adulthood, and those lessons made me the confident, bold woman I am today.

Carol Dweck, a Stanford University researcher on what she calls "fixed" and "growth" mindsets, deeply influenced Duckworth's concept of grit. Dweck found that students who tackled challenges with enthusiasm and curiosity – a learning goal orientation – believed that they could become smarter and more successful if they persisted when tempted to give up. Students with a "fixed" mindset did not hold those same beliefs, and they often quit if they thought that goal failure would threaten their esteem in their own eyes or the eyes of others. Dweck discovered that adding "yet" to student feedback when they made a mistake ("You don't have the skills to get that right yet" versus "You are wrong") encouraged them to try again and build a growth mindset. "Goals gone wild" and its emphasis on performance outcomes over learning goals is very similar to the ideas of Dweck's mindset definitions, and they both show how the pursuit of one's goals with open-minded curiosity is the best approach.

"I Killed the Tiger"

In May 2017, documentary filmmaker Nisha Pahuja was traveling in her native India, following the efforts of two organizations that educated men and boys about the biases and opinions they might have about women's inferiority to men. That's when she saw news reports of the brutal rape of a 13-year-old girl by three older men, including a cousin whose wedding she was attending when the crime occurred. Pahuja decided to switch her focus to covering what happened to the girl and her family when they sought justice. This is the subject of her riveting documentary *To Kill a Tiger*, which was nominated for a 2024 Academy Award.

Watching the deft intermingling of scenes from the lush, but impoverished, farming community in Jharkland's eastern province with the stark, ugly reality "Kiran" (not her name) and her family face from their village when they stand with their daughter against the rapists, is a beautiful illustration of a concept I call "relational grit." I believe we grow this type of grit through positive interactions with people who know and support our big, hard goals; their words and actions cause us to become braver, grittier, and more committed than if they were not in our corner.

Kiran's father, Ranjit, is depicted in the film as a tortured but resolute man who is willing to battle against the country's degrading culture toward women (a female is raped every 16 minutes and the attacks often go unreported), antiquated justice systems that are slow to act or punish men (many in the village thought Kiran should marry one of the rapists to bring peace to the community), and the fact that very few fathers take the public position of supporting a daughter's desire to see rapists brought to justice.

The family was often cloistered in their home because they were shunned by their village, and the parents feared harm coming toward them and their children if they ventured out alone. It is in these dim, candle-lit scenes that you see moving conversations between Ranjit and his wife about what they are willing to endure despite poverty, social isolation, and occasional uncertainty.

We also witness the silent, determined face of Kiran as she paints her fingernails and toenails bright pink, and then repeats the facts of her assault repeatedly late at night at her father's gentle encouragement, so that she will have the confidence to be unflinching and calm when she comes face-to-face with her attackers in the small court-room. It is the faces of the family members as these scenes play out, and the obvious love and respect they have for each other, that seem to empower Kiran as the trial date nears. This is relational grit at its best, and it's something we should all have in our lives – especially when we pursue difficult goals.

The country was "stunned" in 2018, 14 months after the violent attack, when Judge Diwakar Pandey's landmark decision found the three rapists guilty, sentencing them to 25 years in jail. The final scenes of the movie show Kiran's family enjoying a night at a local carnival, the children screaming in delight on rides and enjoying treats that were usually unaffordable for them. A smile wreathing his deeply creased face, Ranjit has the satisfied look of someone who took on the impossible and won.

"They told me I couldn't kill a tiger," he said. "Well, I killed the tiger."

Since the ruling, India is seeing a rise in young girls coming forward with the support of their fathers to report sexual assaults. Pahuja reflected on Kiran's courage and the impact of the case in an interview: "I'm so proud that reports of assaults have gone up pre-cipitously since Kiran shared her story. It really speaks to her power and to what Ranjit represents in terms of how crucial male allyship is to helping keep women safe."

- ◆ Whose authentic grit has inspired you to pursue a big goal?
- ◆ Has your own display of this type of good grit changed some-one else's belief in what they can accomplish with passion and persistence?
- ◆ What relationships do you have that bolster your confidence and help you believe in your ability to do hard things?
- ◆ What situations and places have that type of positive effect on you and how often do you experience them? Is it enough or do you need to find ways to get more of them?

Amabots, Tattletales, and Purposeful Darwinism

If you were to clone two of the earliest productivity enthusiasts who believed in pushing people to their emotional and physical limits by using data to enforce their efficiency – Frederick Winslow Taylor and Henry Ford – and bring them back to life in the twenty-first century, you would probably create two of the world's richest men: Jeff Bezos, the founder of Amazon, and Elon Musk, the co-founder of SpaceX and Tesla.

Like Taylor and Ford, Bezos and Musk are praised as visionary innovators who have made the world more efficient while changing our perception of where we can travel and how we will do it. But they also share the appalling belief that pushing people to their physical and emotional limits to make as much money as possible is an acceptable way to do business. (All four have also been accused of seeing workers as "robots," although at Amazon they are called "Amabots.")

Bezos is unapologetic about how Amazon drives its employees to their limits to boost profits and make the stock soar. A 2015 *New York Times* exposé of the company's bruising management practices detailed Amazon's workplace norms, expectations, and the 14 "values" that workers must recite on demand. The article reported that people were expected to work late and even on vacations, and were encouraged to tattle on each other with secret feedback to others' bosses because "harmony is overvalued." One former employee told the reporter that his main memory of his time at Amazon was seeing men and women crying at their desks. "You walk out of a conference room, and you'll see a grown man covering his face," Bo Olson recalled.

This is the "purposeful Darwinism" of the company, which fires people receiving the lowest rankings, including those with cancer or women recovering from miscarriages who took time off to recover (see the Kantor and Streitfeld article, "Inside Amazon," *New York Times*, August 15, 2015). It took media scrutiny for Amazon to install air conditioning in a Pennsylvania warehouse where temperatures went as high as 100°, and where ambulances were lined up ready to whisk away workers who collapsed. Employees describe an environment of constant combat and sniping akin to the television show *Survivor*, and women – who are barely represented in top leadership roles – say that the criteria for promotion rewards behavior like giving aggressive feedback, which punishes them unfairly because of the penalty they pay for violating gender norms (the "Black Sheep Effect") and acting like stereotypical men.

"Hustle, Hustle, Hustle"

Musk's treatment of workers at Tesla has also come under scrutiny for dangerous work conditions and a refusal to abide by California's restrictions during the early spread of the coronavirus. Defying countywide stay-at-home orders, Musk ordered workers back on the car's production lines in May 2021, resulting in a super-spreader condition with hundreds of cases of coronavirus erupting. His decision-making also came under fire when ambulances were summoned hundreds of times between 2014 and 2018 because of employee fainting spells, dizziness, seizures, abnormal breathing, and chest pain; hundreds of other ambulance visits were due to injuries and medical emergencies. One worker said, "I've seen people pass out, hit the floor like a pancake and smash their face open. They just send us to work around [them] while [they are] still lying on the floor."

Even worse, workers have been left scarred, hospitalized for long periods, and unable to ever work again after being injured by working with toxic materials that they had not been trained to use. Injuries were often belittled by supervisors, according to former employees, and accidents were not recorded to avoid state penalties and scrutiny (https://revealnews.org/article/tesla-says-its-factory-is-saferbut-it-left-injuries-off-the-books/). It was "hustle, hustle, hustle" all the time, one said, usually to meet unrealistic production numbers that Musk was prone to suddenly announce to the public in podcast interviews or social media posts. Alan Ochoa, a former Tesla worker on medical leave, said in 2021 that his superiors "put the production numbers ahead of the safety and well-being of the employees," a situation that fits the definition of "goals gone wild," and that always hurts an organization's reputation or existence, or both.

This doesn't mean that Bezos and Musk haven't left their stamp on the world with their ideas and inventions. In fact, Musk is credited with single-handedly resuscitating the United States space program with his successful moonshot bid of building a private company, SpaceX, that puts ordinary people into space and carries out successful government missions. But both men and their efforts to disrupt thinking about how problems get solved are also a cautionary tale of what can go wrong when the pursuit of a big dream with passion and perseverance at all costs leaves a trail of pain and destruction in its wake – something I call "stupid grit."

Stupid grit is the obstinate pursuit of a long-term goal that presents more negatives than positives because circumstances have changed. People with this type of bad grit are arrogant and believe that they don't need to seek or heed advice from others because they are certain that they know best. Their lack of humility and unwillingness to learn from others, or be seen as wrong, can torpedo their goals and destroy years of work. When taken to an extreme, stupid grit can kill.

- When have you had stupid grit?
- What will you do to avoid stupid grit?
- Has someone else's stupid grit impacted you? If so, how can you minimize these types of people and situations in your life?

"I Don't Have a Quit Button"

Serena Williams, the legendary Black athlete who learned to play tennis on the shabby courts of Compton, California, and who overcame racism to become the top competitor in what was once an exclusively White person's sport, is thought to be the greatest women's player of all time. She revolutionized the game with a mix of aggressive play, powerful strokes, and tenacity to win 23 Grand Slam titles while holding the world's number-one ranking for 319 weeks.

Her drive to be the best meant she didn't always have the best judgment about competing with illness and injuries. "I have a stopping issue," she told a reporter in 2015. "I don't have a quit button. You just can't press control-alt-quit with me. I do not know when to quit." To solve this problem, Williams trusted her family and training team to keep her from pushing herself to and beyond extreme limits, and she listened even when she didn't want to. Her humility is something that is embedded in good grit, because humility shows that you are coachable, willing to listen to others, and can be made aware of your limitations.

- Do you listen to people who warn you that you are being rash or impulsive in your goal pursuit?
- Do you reach out and ask for their help when you think you might need a different perspective?

> Two types of humility make up good grit. Intellectual humility is composed of curiosity, openness to new ideas, and the willingness and desire to learn from others. It is characterized by confidence that lacks conceit. Social humility is called the "social lubricant" because it builds relationships that stand the test of time. Also, people don't believe they will be taken advantage of in a relationship that has social humility, which makes cooperation more likely.

WeFailed

If you have lived or traveled anywhere near a big city anywhere in the world in the last 15 years, you have probably seen the WeWork logo on a building. At one point the company boasted 466,000 members working out of 485 locations in more than 100 cities in 28 countries. In 2019, the company's charismatic founder, Adam Neumann, sat atop a company valued at $47 billion that he was convinced would "change the consciousness" of the world through WeLiving, WeLearn and other We-themed spinoffs. His capacity to generate enthusiasm among investors and people who believed that he was more than just a real estate company leasing space to tenants, but that he had "superpowers" that would transform the way the world gathered, was eye-opening.

From the time Neumann co-founded the company in 2010 with an architect, to its spectacular implosion under the weight of his bizarre behavior, drug and alcohol use, aggressive self-dealing and imperialist tendencies in 2019, Neumann was a study in two types of bad grit – "faux grit" and "selfie grit." Faux grit is behavior where a person pretends to themselves or others that they have achieved difficult things, but they have taken shortcuts or faked those accomplishments to obtain admiration and other advantages. Instead of being an astute businessman whose success was solid, scrutiny of their accounting methods showed that the company was a house of cards marked by fake, dishonest practices.

Selfie grit is relentless self-promotion that fails to credit the contributions of people who assisted you in your goal pursuit. One of Neumann's enduring bitter legacies is that his greed and self-absorption earned him tens of millions of dollars and a lavish lifestyle that continues to this day. But the employees who had bought into his dream and worked for a pittance were left with crushed dreams and worthless stock options.

- Have you ever exhibited selfie grit by achieving a hard goal, but failed to credit the people who had your back or played a role in your success?
- Have you ever inflated your accomplishments because you wanted other people to admire you, but you didn't do the work that was required?
- If the answer to either one of these questions is "yes," what are the behaviors and qualities you can cultivate that will help you avoid these tendencies going forward? Bad grit repels others, and positive relationships are required to achieve hard goals, so pinpoint what you need to work on, if necessary, whether it's exhibiting more interest in other people and their goals, acting grateful for the help you receive from others, or being more honest and humble. Efforts made in these directions will pay big dividends in your life and in your goal pursuit.

Climbers often freeze or fall to their deaths while either attempting to reach a mountain summit or descending shortly after achieving that big goal. This is often blamed on "summit fever," a mixture of bad judgment brought on by not getting enough oxygen to their brains, and stupid grit. While numerous documentaries have told these tragic stories about how bad luck, poor judgment, and suspect motives often led a climber to their death, *Torn* is a documentary that shows the impact on the family and surviving children of Alex Lowe, considered one of the greatest climbers of all time, who lost his life chasing the risky goal of being one of the first people to ski down the Shishapangma in Tibet. The film is by explorer Max Lowe, who was 10 when his father died, and it is a poignant glimpse into the legacy left behind when survivors mourn the impact of a loved one's risk-taking in extreme conditions, and the questions they are left with about whether or not the "high" of the thrill was greater than the love Alex Lowe felt for his children.

All Play and No Work Equals Zero Grit

Few experiments are as well-known as psychologist Walter Mischel's famous "Marshmallow Test," which rewarded preschoolers who had the ability to wait 15 minutes for a second treat after being given one marshmallow. His longitudinal study comparing the children who could wait versus the ones who could not established findings that having self-control, also called self-regulation or willpower, conferred multiple benefits in life. High self-control at the age of four predicted better grades, higher teacher evaluations, lack of substance abuse problems, better standardized test scores, excellent leadership evaluations, and greater popularity through one's teens. As time went on, early self-control led to more career success, better educational outcomes, and fewer divorces and relationship problems.

Having the ability to delay gratification is central to cultivating grit. Being able to say "no" to oneself when tempted to blow off work in order to have fun, overindulge in alcohol, skip sports workouts, and avoid discomfort through procrastination is a behavior you must master. If you have big dreams that will involve intensive planning, financial sacrifice, and multiple challenges, you will have to find a way to build willpower if that is a struggle of yours.

In the last 20 years, some of the most popular recommendations to build willpower when you feel like giving in to temptation to avoid doing hard things have included ingesting a teaspoon of sugar, watching movies of people who portray self-control, and being around others who possess willpower. Some of these studies have not been replicated, so here are the best recommendations experts currently endorse for building self-control:

- **Imagine yourself as someone who has high self-control.** Many people advise playing the game of "acting as if" or pretending to be a character in a movie to try on willpower and see how it feels. Sometimes it is our belief in our ability to withstand temptation that can make the difference in giving up or staying on course.
- **Avoid alcohol.** The moment you remove the ability to have complete control over withstanding temptation, which alcohol is notorious for doing, you are in trouble.

- **Pick one area of your life where you want to instill more discipline.** It could be in starting a program of walking 8,000 steps five times a week or cutting out desserts on weekdays. Research has found that building up willpower in one area of your life, and not suddenly trying to improve self-control in multiple areas (something that usually dooms New Year's resolutions by the third Monday of January, called "Blue Monday" partly because people feel like failures because of broken resolutions), can improve willpower across multiple areas.

- **Remind yourself constantly of your big goals.** Use computer screensavers, a vision board that you put in a key location, and written messages on sticky notes that are placed in various spots: your car's steering wheel, the bathroom mirror, or a briefcase. These notes "prime" you to think goal-directed thoughts that will prompt the behavior you desire. In *Creating Your Best Life* I came up with the idea of changing computer passwords to reflect your goals, and to obtain a vanity license plate that spells out your big goal in seven letters. Your creativity can be very valuable when it comes to priming your environment.

- **Choose your friends wisely.** Being around people who are also pursuing big goals, and who are finding ways to build their own muscle of self-control, can have a contagious effect on you.

- **Create an "implementation intention" that pairs an environmental cue with an action that you want to take.** Peter Gollwitzer found that when you decide ahead of time that you will connect something like the clock striking three with doing 10 pushups – called "if-then" scenarios – you will triple your likelihood of accomplishing hard goals.

A study published in the *British Journal of Health Psychology* found that college students who went from being non-exercisers to working out two to three times per week reported a decrease in stress, smoking, alcohol and caffeine consumption,

(continued)

an increase in healthy eating and maintenance of household chores, and better spending and study habits. Two months later, the students did better on lab tests of willpower. The researchers concluded that saying "yes" to doing something hard when you want to say "no" teaches you to remain calm and poised in the face of difficulty, whether it means saying no to drinking, managing stress more effectively, or studying more.

Do You Have "Anticipation of a Hassle?"

In the year before I found the MAPP program, I was casting about for a place to learn about the science behind goal success, which took me to the Albert Ellis Institute in New York City. Ellis was the founder of Rational Emotive Behavioral Therapy, a disruption to conventional therapy approaches. His many bestselling books, including *A Guide to Rational Living* and *How to Make Yourself Happy*, outlined his belief that how you perceive the world controls your behavior, and that when you change your thoughts, you change your life.

One of the experts he brought to his Institute in the summer of 2004 was Dr. William Knaus, who was described as the world's expert on procrastination, and the co-author with Ellis of *Overcoming Procrastination*. Ellis believed that procrastination stemmed from irrational and magical thinking that led to counterproductive procrastination activities. I found the day to be transformative because it simplified procrastination into an understandable set of thoughts and behaviors that I could control.

The most life-changing advice I got that day was to become aware of the impact of having a mindset called "Anticipation of Hassle." When you "anticipate a hassle" instead of getting started on goal pursuit, it means that you are suddenly imagining the "hassle" you will have to go through if you want to do something like investigate a master's program to enroll in, and instead of getting started, you begin a narrative in your mind about how you're going to be confused about the offerings and different universities, and then you will have to spend a lot of time on the phone talking to people to clarify your questions, and then the applications will be too long for you to fit into your schedule, and then you'll have to apply for financial aid and that is going to be such a hassle that you might as well not even look. Get the picture? When you anticipate a hassle, you never get started.

◆ Does the idea of anticipating a hassle ring a bell with you? Have you quit working on the steps of a goal because you "anticipated a hassle" and put it off until another day, but then you anticipated a hassle the next time, too, and ultimately didn't make any progress? What would you tell yourself the next time you see this happening to you?

Growing Your Grit for Goals

Now that you understand that big goals require that you have a set of behaviors and thinking that will help your goal pursuit, go through this chapter's questions and consider all the scenarios that will require that you exhibit passion, withstand temptation, and develop ways to keep going despite discouragement, setbacks, and pessimistic thinking. Other people will play a role in helping you to become gritty, as you saw in the story told in *To Kill A Tiger* about building grit by being in relationships where you become more confident and committed because of the support and actions of the people around you.

Finally, we are close to crossing the BRIDGE to your future, which is the last step in your goal setting journey. This is where you clarify the standards that you are seeking to attain in your big goal. Just like anything else, pursuing an extreme version of excellence can create more problems than pluses. But we must have a bull's-eye on what "challenging and specific" means for our learning and performance goals if we are seeking "best" outcomes in something, and we also need to know when "good enough" in a task is all we need to keep moving forward.

CHAPTER 10

Excellence

Earning Two Crowns a Week

Last year I invested in an Oura ring at the encouragement of a neighbor. It is a wearable device that provides enormous amounts of daily data about physical activity, blood pressure, heart rate, recovery resilience, your personal stress index, and harmful noise in your environment – not to mention every aspect of sleep quality you could ever want.

These and other tiny sensor-rich, wearable computers provide so much feedback about how your body is performing that many professional athletes' costs are underwritten by their teams because they can alert the user, trainers, and coaches that an athlete is overheating, missing too much sleep, recovering slowly, or having unusual blood pressure spikes that can be addressed through a changed diet, an adjusted workout schedule, or instruction in diaphragm breathing.

It's no surprise that all my CEO clients also have Oura rings or smart watches to track their health because they understand that being clear-headed and energized is as important to their professional success as tracking their organizations' productivity. In fact, one client saw in her watch's dashboard feedback that her cortisol levels had spiked and her breathing had gotten shallow during a tense negotiation, so we added new goals to our coaching work so that she could cultivate different behavioral tools to use in similarly stressful situations.

Recently I ran into the neighbor who recommended the Oura ring and I told her how helpful its data had been to me. I noted that it had even been my first sign that I had developed COVID-19 because my temperature had inexplicably risen by a degree one day, and even though I felt fine at the time, a test had immediately confirmed the virus, and I was able to change my plans long before I would have learned I had it otherwise.

I then asked how the device was helping her with her health.

"I try to get two crowns a week," she responded.

"Crowns?" I said, puzzled. "What are crowns?"

She explained the significance of the crowns, which appear over your sleep score when you get an 85 or above on the dashboard. Later, I scrolled backward through months of my results and noticed that I'd never earned more than an average of four crowns a month, which made me set a new goal for myself of measuring my sleep quality by trying to get six a month – fewer than my neighbor – but still a good performance goal for me. (Since I had the data on the days when I did get above an 85, I had an instant checklist telling me what to do if I wanted to achieve that goal.)

If I hadn't engaged in that random friendly conversation when I passed my neighbor on the street, I doubt I would have shot for any type of excellence with my sleep quality – which is now said to be among the most important pieces of data any of us should chart for overall well-being and mental clarity. It woke me up to the fact that as much as I talk about goals, set goals, and think I'm living up to my word about their importance, I can still allow small details like this to escape notice, and can instead gather data, but not use it to measure progress toward a specific, important goal.

Since that conversation, I have begun to adjust little things during the day that will get me closer to hitting my crown goal, like taking five-minute meditation breaks at noon, and beginning my bedtime transition much earlier than I once thought was necessary. Although I'm not golfer Matt Fitzpatrick, I can agree with one of his observations: stats don't lie.

Goals Without Feedback Are Meaningless

Daniel Kahneman, the Nobel Prize winner, noted in an interview a year before his death that one of the greatest advances he'd witnessed during his career was the invention of wearables, like the

Oura ring, and bracelets that track women's periods. He said that the advent of the iPhone in 2008 had revolutionized how psychologists gathered real-time data from the people he studied, making it easier to gauge results and draw accurate conclusions.

As we consider how we define and pursue excellence in our goals, Kahneman's observations about wearables drive home the important message that whenever possible, we need to have accurate feedback about what we are doing to move toward a specific outcome so that we can adjust, amplify, or abandon our approach. A well-known statement in the goal setting world that doesn't have specific attribution is "Goals without feedback, and feedback without goals, are both meaningless."

◆ What is the excellent outcome you are seeking in your goal? Why is it "excellent" to you?

Beware the Peloton

I am not a biker of any kind. When my husband goes away on mountain biking expeditions with his friends, he comes back bruised but exuberant. A Hall of Fame lacrosse player who had competed through pain for years because of a high school wrestling accident that took one of his ACL tendons, an exercise bike had become his best friend after mid-life knee replacement, but I had never liked it. I had my own athletic pursuits, and I knew how to set and pursue measurable goals in those sports.

Then we invested in a Peloton bike. Its huge, inviting screen featuring dozens of interactive workouts from cycling to yoga beckoned to me, so one morning I decided to try a 20-minute cycling class. A novice to this activity, I was doing my best to keep up with the instructor's peppy non-stop orders to stand up, cycle faster, and add more resistance, and I was drenched in sweat and gasping for air when my husband walked into our home gym.

"What's your ranking?" he asked as he peered at the screen. "Oh, you're #194 right now."

He patted me on the back as he turned to walk out. "I was #3 in my class yesterday."

He knows me well enough to know that his comment was enough to spark my competitive juices. I amped up my resistance, stood up off the seat, and I heaved my way through the rest of the class, watching my number slowly climb from 194, to 164, to 121, and finally to 111. When the class ended, I lay down on the floor and gulped water before I limped out, wondering why we had bought a machine that could make me so miserable.

Cycling Gone Wild

In the blink of an eye, I had taken a learning goal of getting accustomed to a new machine that I hoped would bring me pleasure, to a medieval torture device, all because I had turned it into a performance goal when someone said something that challenged me. It took me a week to stop hurting from the pounding I put my knees through, but I had clearly created a goals gone wild scenario that took a learning goal and turned it into a performance goal, and had changed my definition of excellence from curiosity about how the bike worked to trying to rank higher in a class of anonymous screen names.

The next time I got on the Peloton, I knew exactly what I wanted to get from my experience – a fun, cardiovascular workout – and my measurement of excellence was whether or not my heart rate hit the right zone for enough time, if I felt tired but not achy when I finished, and if I had fun listening to the music and the instructor's patter.

Notice that I didn't adopt my neighbor's crown goal when we chatted about our experiences with the Oura ring data, but her comments did make me aware that I shouldn't just accumulate data for data's sake – some people call this "data trash" – and think I'm benefitting enough from the investment. My crown goal suits me right now, I can see I'm making good changes, and I feel the impact of those changes. Now I'm paying more attention to the other data instead of just seeing it without scrutiny, I have new, measurable goals around my stress index, and I'm taking action to bring that more in line with how I want to live.

But my interaction with my husband, Haywood, was a different matter. His opinion of me is important, and I must have wanted to impress him by getting a better score, so my behavior went from curious to crazed as the result of one quick interaction. Instead of trying to get to my "ideal self," I moved into a state called my "should self," because I incorrectly thought that his goal should be my goal, even though it hadn't crossed my mind that I should pay attention to the numbers on the screen at all!

Be careful in your own goal pursuit to know what excellence means to you, and be on the lookout for the people and situations who might trigger you to change what you are trying to pursue so that it fits what they think is an excellent outcome.

◆ Is there anyone in your environment who might cause you to change your definition of excellence because of their role in your life, and your respect or admiration for them?

The Fine Line Between Pushing and Prompting

The story of how 14-year-old Katie Ledecky changed her own definition of excellence in a big goal is now well-known. Her coach at the time, Yuri Suguiyama, took Ledecky out for a meal – something he routinely did with his athletes – and he asked her what her biggest goal was for her swimming that season.

Ledecky thought for a moment. She was in the eighth grade and had never competed outside of the United States and had never even made a cut to compete in the Olympic Trials. "Make the Olympic team?" she answered, looking at him for his affirmation.

"Try again," he responded. "Is that really the best goal you could achieve this year?"

She thought again. "Win the Olympics?" she finally said.

"Say it again," Suguiyama said. She did. It became their secret agreement that day.

When Ledecky made the US 2012 Olympic team at the country's swim trials the following year, the 15-year-old rising high school freshman was the country's youngest Olympic competitor. And when she won the 800-m freestyle event in London in a thrilling showdown in the middle of the pool with the defending British world champion, Rebecca Adlington, Ledecky launched a domination of distance freestyle events that continues to this day, making her the greatest female swimmer of all time, and the winningest female US Olympic athlete.

(The inclusion for the first time of the mile in the 2021 Tokyo Olympics is thought to be the direct result of Ledecky's thrilling assault on the record books, and how much excitement she has brought to making the world see that women are easily as capable of doing long events in the pool as men are.)

There is a fine line between pushing a person to adopt an unrealistic, unsuitable goal that is more reflective of that person's ambitions than the person who is setting the goal. Suguiyama walked that tightrope brilliantly because of his intimate familiarity with Ledecky's mental strength, training capacity, and ability to do things others couldn't do. In his pushback to Ledecky, he was asking her to make sure that the potential excellence he saw in her matched a vision that she could challenge herself to adopt.

Note that he didn't set her goal for her; he asked her a question that allowed her to reflect on what she believed she was capable of. His instincts were right. She has said in subsequent interviews that after that lunch, she never saw anything in her mind except standing atop the Olympic podium.

♦ Who is the mentor, or "persuasive other" (Bandura's term for a person who can help build a person's self-efficacy because of the trust between them) in your life, who would be a good person to possibly challenge you on what "excellence" looks like for you?

How Your Values Can Impact Your Excellence

I've seen in decades of coaching people that the most powerful examples of excellence in goal pursuit usually include a person's top values. For example, one of my clients is the head of the legal department of an international company, and her top VIA strength is "kindness." When we established her annual goals, she said one of them was to develop a team of leaders who would be kind to each other, bucking the cut-throat behavior in some of the company's other departments.

She established metrics for judging whether this behavior was happening, including asking people in their performance reviews if they had assisted their peers with their work when needed, and if anyone had helped them during difficult deadlines or personal crises with research, writing, or bringing a contract to completion. She also rewarded evidence of kindness in the bonus system, and her weekly division meetings always began with an opportunity to share witnessing someone's act of kindness to another person. When the company's engagement scores were tallied by an outside organization, my client was gratified to hear from the CEO that not only had her department scored the highest, the number-one word used to describe their interactions with people across all divisions was "kind."

◆ How do your top strengths show up in your definitions of "excellence"? One of my top strengths is creativity, so it's no surprise that my standard of "excellence" in writing this book is that it is an innovative and compelling approach to goal setting that evokes creativity in people who read it.

Checklist for Excellence

This last step of the BRIDGE method asks that you establish an outcome for your big goal that elicits the feelings of pride, satisfaction, and happiness that can only come from going outside your comfort zone in pursuit of a meaningful, hard goal. Jessica Tracy, a professor at the University of British Columbia, researches the differences between "authentic pride" which comes from pursuing and achieving goals that create confidence, strengthen relationships, and result in more continuous, meaningful achievements, and "hubristic pride," which can destroy relationships with narcissistic behavior like arrogance and conceit. Authentic pride is linked to behaviors like extraversion, conscientiousness, and the ability to get along with others, while hubristic pride can come from a desire to dominate and intimidate others to achieve greater status.

Here's a checklist for pursuing the type of excellence that creates authentic pride, positive outcomes, and personal growth:

◆ Practice self-reflection to assess the reasons for your success to ensure they are attributed to effort and controllable variables
◆ Remain humble and acknowledge the role others play in your positive outcomes

- ◆ Seek accurate feedback that includes constructive criticism to maintain a realistic self-perception
- ◆ Cultivate empathy to avoid self-centered behavior
- ◆ Focus on personal growth rather than dominating others
- ◆ Maintain the perspective that success and achievements can be transitory, and that it does not dictate your self-worth
- ◆ Celebrate others' successes and practice *firgun* – a Yiddish word – which translates to joy in another person's joy
- ◆ Practice gratitude to improve well-being, build relationships, and remain grounded

When we pursue meaningful goals by going through the BRIDGE prompts and are thorough in the creation of an action plan that clearly defines the right type of measurable excellence, we have crossed the bridge from having a dream to being active agents in the designing of our best life.

- ◆ When was the last time you experienced "authentic pride" because of something you did? Describe the goal, who helped you, and what else led to that emotion. Who did you celebrate with?
- ◆ After this experience, did you find it easier to pursue more actions that brought about this type of pride?

> "One person in pursuit of excellence raises the standards of everyone around them. And as they strive for greatness they bring out the greatness in others."
>
> *Jon Gordon*

"My Goal Is My Gift to My Kids"

Denis Crean is a barrel-chested 63-year-old open water swimmer who swam across the 21-mile wide English Channel in August 2023 in a little more than 12 hours with three of his children serving as his crew. It wasn't his first major open water undertaking; he won the

2004 Tampa Bay Marathon Swim in 9-plus hours, swam 28.5 miles around Manhattan Island, swam the Catalina Channel in 16 hours, and is one of the few Triple Crown Open Water and Ice Mile swimmers in the world.

I know Denis through Masters Swimming in the D.C. area, and because of the organization he founded – WaveOne – to teach people how to use open water swimming as a way to harmonize their energy with the natural force of water and have a spiritual experience that changes their lives.

In my interview with Denis, I was curious about how he defined "excellence" when it came to tackling a goal as big and impressive as swimming in the dark, cold water of the English Channel for more than 12 hours – a feat that many have dreamt about, trained for over many years, but still not achieved for reasons ranging from fitness to the tides. His answer surprised me.

"The excellence isn't just about finishing something this big – because I will always fight to finish, if possible," he laughed. "My goal is my gift to my children. I wanted them to see that you can dream big dreams, go for them, and then accomplish hard things with your own effort. That's excellence to me because knowing that, seeing it, and doing it yourself is life-changing."

Denis underscored how the role of others can factor into one's definition of goal excellence. He wasn't swimming to impress his children or anyone else – or even to win, either. He was pursuing his massive English Channel crossing goal **for** his children as a gift to enlarge their perspective on how they can view themselves and their own possibilities in life.

The BRIDGE Across the Channel

Denis's Channel swim is a perfect example of how to use the BRIDGE methodology to go through the steps of establishing a goal pursuit plan, and to shoot for a standard that means excellence to you. Here's how it broke down for him:

- ◆ **Big Goal:** To Swim the English Channel
- ◆ **Type of Goal:** Performance Goal (he had done several big open water swims but had to learn specifics about the Channel and its crossing schedules for some new learning)

- **Brainstorming:** Denis researched who had done it to find out how much training was required, how he would fit it into his schedule, what he would have to consider that younger male swimmers wouldn't have to worry about, how he would handle different challenges that would be sure to arise during the training and the swim itself, etc.

- **Relationships:** He had to hire a captain to oversee his crossing three years ahead of time, train with other swimmers who would be willing to do long swims, ask his children to be the crew that kept him on track and fed him during the swim, tell the people who would believe in his goal and hold him accountable to keep moving toward it, etc.

- **Investments:** He had to pay for a slot to cross the Channel, invest in coaching to help him lower his stroke count per minute to reduce wear and tear on his shoulder, hire nutritionists and other body workers to work on alignment and overuse injuries, buy plane tickets to and from England, etc.

- **Decision-Making:** Because Denis is very focused on finishing whenever he starts an open water event, he relies on trusted people to tell him when to start a crossing to match favorable tides, what side of the pace boat to swim on to prevent accidents or swimming unnecessary mileage, whether he should delay a swim because of illness or a weather issue, when to back off on training to avoid burnout, etc. He relies on curiosity when making the big decisions about what his next open water challenge will be and explores in his mind questions about whether it feels like the right challenge, what it would mean to succeed, and if it would help him grow as a man, a father, and a leader.

- **Good Grit:** Denis goes into each swim understanding that it will be hard, and that the preparation will require swimming when he doesn't want to, fighting off fatigue during the training and the swim itself, and overcoming a desire to quit whenever life interferes with his plans and creates obstacles that look insurmountable. To conquer these types of expected emotions and feelings, Denis has learned to challenge himself to swim just 60 more strokes and then reassess his negative thoughts or do something else in small chunks to distract himself. During the English Channel swim, he knew he needed to swim through the night until dawn, so with every breath, he looked into the sky at Orion's Belt and fixated on how it gradually slipped from view, indicating that he was getting closer to completing the entire swim.

♦ **Excellence:** Denis's overarching goal was to complete the swim across the Channel, and he prepared himself to achieve the goal by measuring improvement in things like training volume, reducing stroke count per minute, and getting the right nutrition to remain hydrated and energized. But excellence also meant how it would inspire his children if they saw him go through his training and the swim, and how that could positively impact them. He also said that if he did all of the work that was required to be ready for the swim – mentally and physically – but the captain called off the swim because of dangerous conditions, he would still classify the ultimate outcome as excellent because he would have done everything within his power to complete the goal.

Good Enough Is Sometimes Good Enough

Even though this book has been filled with references to doing hard things, creating challenging and specific – not easy – goals, and being gritty in pursuit of the type of excellent outcome that will make you proud, it's important to note that there will be times when the steps we will need to take in the process of achieving our goal will not need to be hard or outside our comfort zone. These occasions will usually occur in two situations: when you need to simply accomplish a subgoal that is necessary to keep moving forward with a bigger goal, or when your confidence is shaken from a big setback or loss that has rocked your world.

Barry Schwartz is a professor at Swarthmore University who studied what he calls "the paradox of choice." This occurs when a person is confronted with so many choices about doing something that they either make no choice or they select something they've chosen before because it's easy. He discovered that when shoppers were confronted with 3 types of jam to sample and buy, or 11, they overwhelmingly bought jam when they had fewer choices.

He called this "satisficing" versus "maximizing." When people "satisfice," they don't feel compelled to make the best choice – they just need to make one that allows the task to be completed. When people are trying to make the "best" decision and they contemplate many options, they either make no decision or they make a decision that doesn't fulfill them.

If people have experienced a big setback in their pursuit of a goal, and their confidence is low because of that loss, resilience research has found that they might need to set a "low" goal that isn't hard but getting that win will create feelings of mastery and the confidence to get back in the game.

Gary Latham's research on breaking huge goals into subgoals to build confidence when motivation flags supports these conditions, as well. So as you develop your goal plan through the BRIDGE prompts and do your careful review of relationships, investments, risk-taking, decision-making, grit, and excellence, don't forget that sometimes you will just need to keep going, and notching a win toward a bigger excellent goal is what you will need to do.

- ◆ Write down a time when you needed to do something "easy" to keep a big goal on track. Denis Crean told me that when he felt like he was overtraining and stale during pool swims, he would go to the beach and just paddle around in the ocean and have fun. When I've been stuck too long writing a chapter and I'm in a rut, I switch to writing a fun part of a different chapter, or dictating it in a voice to text app to get me away from a computer screen.

Your Journey Across the BRIDGE

I am now sending you out to make your dreams happen because you have walked across the BRIDGE with me, and you are probably feeling more optimistic, clear, and energized because you understand goal setting science in a new way, and you can see why your previous goal efforts have fallen short. You also have fresh ideas about how to deal with setbacks so that they don't stop you, they become stepping stones. And you are not just imagining what an excellent outcome looks like, you are seeing yourself for the first time in your mind's eye with confidence because even if it feels "unrealistic," you now know that unrealistic goals can cause people to not just do amazing things, they can change the possibilities envisioned by the people around you.

Walk Someone Else Across the BRIDGE

The greatest gift you can give to others, and to me, is for you to share these teachings and tools with people who have never heard of them. If you see one of your children's teachers or coaches talk about SMART goals, buy them a copy of this book to educate them about a better way to formulate goal plans. If you have an opportunity to work in a setting where people feel hopeless, share one of the tools in this to start them on a step-by-step journey to a different life. If you work in an organization that practices using Objectives and Key Results (OKRs) and Key Performance Indicators (KPIs), don't throw the whole system out; consider using Locke and Latham's goal setting theory to break down one of your goals in a new way. Think about leading a different type of brainstorming approach in the office to a black swan event your organization might face, or create a new decision-making matrix that removes the chance of bias or noise creeping in. I learned a long time ago that you can't keep what you don't give away, and this is your opportunity to do just that in a way that can change the world.

Start anywhere, but please start somewhere. We've waited too long to challenge the ingrained, old-fashioned goal systems that don't reflect the cultural and gender nuances of the twenty-first century world. Data is everywhere so take advantage of the other huge transformations that are happening in the world around us, and be excited that the future can be brighter and more fulfilling, as long as you look up and over the mountains, and keep yourself moving toward the light – holding the hand of someone else who needs your hope and energy.

My heart is with you, and I wish you well now and in your future. I hope that reading this book has had the same impact on you as I experienced when I first learned about goal setting theory in 2005 and I suddenly felt like I had the answer that I'd been seeking to achieving excellence in my life. Nothing has been the same since then, and my wish for you is that nothing will ever be the same again for you, either, starting today and that you go and create your best possible life.

PART III

Supplemental Resources

These resources are designed to help you explore the many topics related to goal setting in this book, and particularly to help amplify the learnings that result from using the BRIDGE methodology to create a goal setting plan. In addition to the question prompts sprinkled throughout different chapters, please use the resources to be as thorough as possible in considering your options. It will be helpful to have a journal or notebook that is completely devoted to what you learn in this book and the results of gathering information and making lists. Please copy the worksheets to use over and over for every new goal you pursue because the techniques here have been tested with many people on many different types of goals, and the BRIDGE approach has stood up to scrutiny.

You may go back and forth from reading chapters to doing worksheets, or you may want to finish the book and then circle back to do the journaling exercises. Some people like the support of a Mastermind group as they prepare their goal plans and get the feedback from trusted allies and friends. Whatever you do, give it your best efforts and take your goals seriously, because the superpower humans possess of being able to imagine a different future and then work toward it is a gift not to be taken lightly.

Note: many of the worksheets may have overlap with another worksheet so that the foundational principles of goal setting theory and the BRIDGE methodology are reinforced, and that is by design. You may prefer one worksheet's focus over another one around topics like decision-making, brainstorming or investments, for example, as each one might have a slightly different emphasis. Flip through them and pick the one that suits where you most want to focus in the creation of your goal strategy. It's better to be thorough and repetitive on these concepts than brief and superficial.

History of Productivity Approaches Since 1870

Frederick Taylor – "Father of Scientific Management." Began field of time-motion studies and discounted importance of worker emotions or well-being. Believed that avoiding wasteful motion by teaching workers was the answer.

Henry T. Ford – "Fordism" was developed to create as many Model T Ford cars as quickly as possible and revolved around redesigning factories to streamline workflow. Worker input was considered irrelevant.

Management by Objectives (MBOs) – Peter Drucker advocated for setting goals collaboratively with workers, but like earlier methods it was heavily quantitative and top-down without flexibility or measurement of softer aspects of change.

Objectives and Key Results & Key Performance Indicators (OKRs and KPIs) – Intel's redesigned MBOs focused on big objectives starting at the top of an organization and then used KPIs to track progress. Downside is they can become misaligned across an organization and fail to measure "softer" metrics like engagement and learning behaviors. This approach can be so rigid that feedback is delayed and pivots don't happen quickly enough, and too many KPIs can lead to information overload and burnout.

George Doran – Management consultant who suggested that SMART goals be specific, measurable, achievable, relevant, and time-bound, but research has found that this is often unsuccessful, simplistic, and can even harm success.

Toyota Productivity System (TPS) – Became popular for "bullet train thinking" and "stretch" goals, but without proper implementation the goals often discouraged workers and led to cheating. Their "just in time" manufacturing system broke down during COVID-19 and companies are now stockpiling "just in case."

Goal Setting Theory – Edwin Locke and Gary Latham published this "open" theory in 1990 about the differences between learning and performance goals, and that both goals have best performance when they are "challenging and specific." Performance is predicted by ability, commitment, feedback, and availability of resources.

Further variables include complexity of the goal, self-efficacy (belief you can do something), persistence, and strategy. This is the most validated, proven theory on motivation and success in academia, yet remains mostly unknown.

Write about the approaches you have used in your goal setting. Did you use any of these systems? Did they work? Who taught them to you?

Values in Action (VIA) Character Strengths Survey

Created by Positive Psychology pioneers Martin Seligman and Chris Peterson, the VIA (Values in Action) Character Strengths Survey is one of the most popular and well-validated strengths tests available in the world today. To date, it has been taken by almost three million men and women in more than 190 countries and has become a leading tool used in a variety of settings from corporations to schools that helps people understand the ways in which they most authentically experience and thrive in the world.

The VIA test doesn't measure weaknesses or deficits; rather, it ranks one's character strengths (such as wisdom, kindness, gratitude, zest, bravery, love of learning, etc.) from 1 to 24.

Research has found that the understanding and use of one's top strengths can not only make people feel more positive, but it can also lead to greater fulfillment and success with one's goals.

Additionally, when people develop their top strengths in new and creative ways, it can have a significant impact on quality of life as well as a positive effect on relationships, careers, and personal growth.

Discussions of strengths also include a look at the ways in which one might overuse or underuse their strengths to their detriment, and how to find new ways to identify and work around difficult challenges using one's strengths more appropriately.

To get started, register for a free account at the VIA Institute website at http://viacharacter.org. The test itself is 120 questions and takes about 15 minutes to complete.

Write your top 5 and bottom 5 VIA strengths below. Do the results feel accurate? Why or why not?

Examples of Strengths Overuse/Underuse

Contrary to some reports, it's not always a good idea to maximize the use of one's top strengths to the exclusion of lesser strengths. More is not always better, something that Aristotle noted several centuries ago when he called for the "golden mean" when pursuing virtues, athletics, or any type of behavior. Courage, he said, was reckless when overused, and cowardice when underused.

Below are examples of how strengths can manifest when they are overused/underused:

Virtue	Overuse	Underuse
Gratitude	Obsequiousness	Thoughtlessness
Wisdom	Overreliance on past	Shallow thinking
Zest	Over-exuberance	Dullness/"Eeyore"
Self-regulation	Lack of spontaneity	Addiction/rashness
Humility	Can't hear/believe praise	Bragging
Love of Learning	Analysis paralysis	Ignorance
Curiosity	Nosiness/Prying	Self-absorption
Kindness	People-pleasing/doormat	Indifference
Courage	Recklessness	Playing it safe
Love & Be Loved	Blindness to others' flaws	Superficial friends
Appreciation of Beauty	Perfectionism	Mediocrity
Judgment	Self-critical/too critical	Poor judgment
Hope/Optimism	Dreamy/Unrealistic	No goals/pessimistic
Teamwork	Too much collaboration	Won't ask for help
Leadership	Dictatorship	Lacks responsibility
Creativity	Too many ideas	Stale thinking
Social Intelligence	Hypersensitive	Oblivious
Forgiveness	Being disrespected	Holding grudges
Humor	Making fun of others	Humorless
Perseverance	Stupid grit	Giving up
Prudence	Editing oneself a lot	Being reckless
Spirituality/purpose	Dogmatic	Aimless
Fairness	Unfairness to oneself/others	Discriminatory
Honesty	Hurtful/Tactless	Evasive

Me at My Best

Take the free VIA Strengths test at www.viacharacter.org and look at your top five strengths. The test will take about 15 minutes. Think of a time, or period, in your life when you had a "peak" experience, made a difference, succeeded at something important, or others told you they admired how you had done something specific. Think of the ways in which your strengths played a role in this experience and write a few paragraphs about it, singling out each one and where you see its role.

Some people have an initial "What?!" reaction to seeing their strengths because we often take our strengths for granted. They feel natural to us, so we easily gravitate toward using them and don't always realize that other people don't see the world the way we do.

When we fail to acknowledge and use our strengths effectively, however, we miss opportunities to be successful and appear authentic to others. One interesting note: a sure sign that you have a top five strength is when you are *offended* by its absence in others. You can't understand how someone else might not be kind, patient, zestful, or curious, to cite a few strengths, because those might be the top prisms through which you see and interact with the world.

Best Possible Future Selves Exercise

Optimism is a powerful tool for increasing happiness and life satisfaction because it boosts positive feelings about the future, increases self-efficacy, and leads to self-fulfilling prophecies. The goal of this exercise is for you to experience the power of hopeful and optimistic thinking, goal commitment, and enhanced zest.

INSTRUCTIONS

Previous research has persuasively shown that writing expressively about oneself and one's feelings has numerous benefits for health, emotional adjustment, hope, and well-being. In this exercise, you will visualize and write about your "best possible future selves." Possible selves are descriptions of yourself living a life in which you have achieved your most cherished goals. This exercise can improve mood, willpower, self-awareness, and enhance priorities. It can also help you "make meaning" of what has come before and assist in defining your purpose and unique strengths and gifts. It can also highlight discrepancies between where you are today and where you would like to be.

HERE ARE YOUR SPECIFIC INSTRUCTIONS:

Visualize your life in the future. Imagine that everything has gone as well as it possibly could. You have worked hard and succeeded at accomplishing all your life goals. Think of this as the realization of all your life dreams. Now, write about what you imagined in great detail.

Do this for 20 minutes per day for three days in a row. Some research indicates that writing on paper, not a computer, involves a deeper structure in the brain that can produce powerful results, so that might be an optimal approach. This is an exercise not necessarily designed to be shared with others, so write freely. If anxiety emerges, try to just jot down words or bullet points. The goal is to complete all three days with as much detail and variety across the days as possible.

Positive ("Wise") Interventions

A seminal paper, "Benefits of Frequent Positive Affect" (2005), is one of the most noteworthy findings from Positive Psychology research. Authored by Laura King, Sonja Lyubomirsky, and Ed Diener, the study summarizes hundreds of all kinds of research to identify the determinants of success across multiple realms of life – health, friendship, career, etc. After considering longitudinal, correlational, causal, and other types of research, the trio concluded that **success across all domains of life is preceded by being in a flourishing place first.** In brief, happiness precedes success; happiness does not follow the achievement of goals.

Accordingly, it isn't possible to responsibly address the topics around goal setting and grit without first discussing its necessary antecedents: positive (or wise) interventions (PIs). These are habits of mind and behavior that have been found to generate emotional flourishing, which has many descriptors, including contentment, joy, pride, happiness, awe, joy, peacefulness, ecstasy, and cheerfulness. Positive emotions have multiple outcomes that are evolutionarily beneficial, and that make it possible for people to succeed in important goals and survive.

For example, Barbara Fredrickson's "Broaden and Build" Theory states that generating and experiencing "micromoments" of well-being causes people to become more curious, prosocial, kind, zestful, and diligent, thus broadening their "thought-action repertoire," while simultaneously making it harder to feel cynicism, bias, pessimism, and hopelessness, among other negative emotions. When people experience positive emotions, they also have greater capacity to "build" strong relationships with other people, which assists them in challenging and sad times, while also building a network of proactive support.

Thousands of studies are coalescing around several behaviors and ways of thinking that enhance well-being for everyone, and even unleash the "undoing effect" of neutralizing negative moods and situations. These PIs are now known as "wise" interventions because some are more suitable to certain types of people than others, and thus generate greater returns after an early investment than other PIs might. To create and sustain a ratio of 5:1 (5 positive emotions or behaviors to 1 negative), which is the ratio most often seen in flourishing work teams, individuals, and couples, one must be "wise" about matching their character strengths to a PI. For example, an individual high in zest might find more positive results from exercise, while another person who has top strengths of judgment and love of learning might prefer to spend time in altruistic activities like teaching adults to read or volunteering for a non-profit like Habitat for Humanity.

Here are the most popular, well-studied PIs that everyone can experiment with and use to prepare for success in one's personal and professional lives. These can have many unique variations that fit your life circumstances, but the most important thing is that you take control of your well-being instead of simply waiting for happiness to arrive.

PROVEN POSITIVE INTERVENTIONS

Meditation: Apps like Calm.com or GetSomeHeadspace.com bring mindfulness to you. As little as seven weeks of short, daily sessions of meditation have been found to alter the brain structure, while also improving emotional regulation, mood, and feelings of joy and peace.

Exercise: All types of movement make a positive difference, but aerobic exercise tends to have a more immediate, lasting impact than activities like lifting weights. Being in nature while exercising is an extra plus that boosts vitality for hours.

Gratitude: Cultivating an attitude of gratitude through exercises like "Three Blessings" and "The Gratitude Visit" are popular. As you count blessings, it becomes easier to notice good things as they occur around you and build a habit of looking for good.

Giving: Altruism is one of the highest forms of morality in many spiritual traditions, but it is also beneficial to anyone who takes the time or resources to give to others. The person who gives has been found to experience the "helper's high." Many people discover that doing random acts of kindness is an easy, optimal way to boost mood.

Music: Listening to music that reminds someone of a positive time in life evokes happy memories, and it's been found that livelier, upbeat music can cause depressed people to think and move more quickly, reversing the sluggishness they experience.

Journaling: Writing down one's thoughts and feelings, and journaling about past experiences, doesn't just improve the immune system, it also helps people to "make meaning" of their lives and see silver linings and positive outcomes from adversity. Blogging has also been found to have a similar impact on well-being.

Using Strengths: Knowing one's top strengths is a PI for people because we often take our unique character strengths for granted. We inaccurately assume that if it comes naturally to us, it must come naturally to others. Understanding how your strengths accentuate and define your "best self" has been found to improve well-being. Other research shows that you must endeavor to use your top strengths every day in new and creative ways to maintain that well-being.

Write down what you know about yourself that improves your mood, optimism and emotional flourishing. Are they different from what is listed here? What new interventions would you like to try to enhance your wellbeing and maximize your chances of goal success?

Why Is Happiness the Rocket Fuel of Success?

In 2005, a meta-analysis of success by three leading researchers, Sonja Lyubomirsky, Ed Diener, and Laura King, concluded that **all success in life is preceded by being happy first – not vice versa.** For this reason, any discussion of goal setting, goal pursuit, and goal success must include the important information that we all need to voluntarily amplify our well-being daily to set the stage for any type of success. While we all have genetic set points for well-being, and some find it easier to generate and savor positive emotions, everyone can rise to the top of their own genetic set point range through the practice of behaviors that have been found to positively impact most people, such as meditation, journaling, the practice of gratitude, and acts of forgiveness.

Top empirical reasons why **success follows** emotional flourishing:

◆ Emotional flourishing promotes superior mental health, including cognitive flexibility and the ability to broaden one's thinking with curiosity and a "growth mindset."

◆ Higher well-being promotes physical health because people are more likely to engage in healthier behaviors like regular exercise, a balanced diet, and good sleep habits.

◆ Happiness brings more hope and optimism, which leads people to persist longer and harder at goal pursuit.

◆ Flourishing people are more likely to build positive relationships with others because they tend to exhibit better interpersonal skills such as empathy, good communication, and generosity.

◆ Happiness reduces anxiety and depression, leading to greater emotional resilience.

◆ When workers experience higher well-being, they have been found to be more engaged, motivated, and focused, leading to greater productivity, increased job satisfaction, more career advancement, and overall success in the workplace.

◆ Increased wellbeing can provide a sense of purpose and fulfillment, leading one to feel greater self-acceptance that leads to self-actualization.

Source: Lyubomirsky, S., King, L., & Diener, E. (2005). The benefits of frequent positive affect: Does happiness lead to success? *Psychological Bulletin* 131(6), 803–855.

Building the Muscle of Self-Efficacy

There are four different ways to build self-efficacy, which is a path to motivation and goal accomplishment that was studied and refined into self-efficacy theory by Dr. Albert Bandura, who has spent most of his adult years in residence at Stanford University as a professor of psychology.

Self-efficacy is one of the four traits of happy people, and those traits can be cultivated. They also include optimism, extraversion, and self-confidence. There are four ways to build self-efficacy, and without self-efficacy, one often cannot pursue important goals that allow one to feel competent, autonomous, and connected to others. That is why self-efficacy is frequently called "the muscle of goal accomplishment."

Here are the ways we can build this important trait:

1. **Mastery experiences.** The most powerful way to build self-efficacy is to break large goals into smaller goals that are then accomplished step-by-step. Confidence arises from methodically taking the steps to develop mastery and skills that allow bigger and more complicated goals to be tackled.

2. **Good stress responses.** People who can respond to difficulties, setbacks, challenges, and failures by restoring their equilibrium with responses like mindfulness techniques, humor, meditation, deep breathing, and other techniques can cope better than those who give up, ruminate, and become pessimistic about their chances of success.

3. **Persuasive other.** We begin to believe in ourselves and our ability to do hard things when someone whom we admire and trust believes in us. This person can be a mentor, role model, teacher, parent, godparent, spiritual leader, or other person who has observed you long enough to have an accurate sense of who you are and what you are capable of.

4. **Proximal role model.** When we can see someone in our environment doing something that we want to do, or who has already accomplished something we long to accomplish, it flattens our learning curve and allows us to visualize ourselves more easily in their shoes. One of the sayings in goal setting is, "You can't hit a target you can't see," so seeing a

role model makes our movement toward the finished product that much easier and gives us a boost of hope.

Recent research has also found that inspirational leaders who are skilled at public speaking have the capacity to inspire enthusiasm, motivation, and self-efficacy in others through persuasive storytelling, powerful visioning, and personal sharing. John F. Kennedy's famous speech about sending a man to the moon with the phrase "We do these things not because they are easy, but because they are hard" is one example of masterful oratory that inspired self-efficacy.

Write below about the people, situations and times when your self-efficacy has been enhanced in the four ways listed above. Do you need to boost your self-efficacy more to prepare yourself for pursuing your big goals? How will you do it?

Performance Goal Checklist

According to goal setting theory by Edwin Locke and Gary Latham, some of the goals we pursue are called "performance goals," which means that we have pursued and successfully achieved those goals before. This means that we can identify the same steps we need to take to succeed again, and in what order, to be able to set a metric of progress, a specific outcome, and the date by which that outcome can be achieved. Locke and Latham found that best results always came from setting "challenging and specific goals," which is defined as goals that are **not** easily accomplished with little effort, and the general assurance that we'll have no trouble succeeding.

Some of our tactics might change slightly to accommodate a new workplace, an updated procedure, or the use of slightly different materials, for example, but a performance goal checklist ought to be usable by others in the event you cannot perform the task yourself. The best checklists are not overly detailed but contain the most important steps of completion. How someone performs the steps might vary, but the building blocks of accomplishment should remain the same.

Before creating your checklist, write down anything that is new or different from previous goal pursuit. Are there any potential obstacles to consider in pursuing the goal that should be discussed or thought through before initiating action? Think these through and write down the appropriate questions that need to be answered and incorporated into the checklist. Next, list every step, including what metric needs to be used to gauge progress toward the best outcome. Always make sure that this list could be easily followed by someone other than yourself.

Add any notes here to clarify an instruction or explain a measurement. Remember: the checklist ought to be so clear that these extra notes are minimal, but if they will impact safety or the excellence of the final product, include them here.

Learning Goal Exercise

Learning goals differ from performance goals because you have yet to either achieve this particular goal or acquire the knowledge to do it in a new way. If you apply performance goal metrics – a specific number of new customers by a specific date, for example – in a learning goal condition, people may try a few solutions that have worked before with other goals but give up out of anxiety, frustration, or hopelessness when they fail.

Learning goals can be "challenging and specific" by creating progress metrics outside your comfort zone. But learning, creativity, innovation, and risk-taking should be emphasized over setting a specific outcome by a specific date. This handout will help you approach your learning goal in an effective, organized, and fun way.

What's the learning goal and why is it a learning goal for you?

What's the importance of this goal?

Where will you get the necessary knowledge or skills to succeed at this goal?

How can you make the acquisition of this knowledge by a certain date challenging and specific, as opposed to vague, or setting a "do your best" condition?

The BRIDGE Methodology

Many goal setting and goal pursuit strategies are well-meaning, but they are often filled with antiquated acronyms like SMART goals, which don't match evidence-based approaches, or they are missing a number of steps that don't reflect the nuances of Locke and Latham's goal setting theory or the newest science around the cultural, psychological, gender-based, and physical differences that we now know impact how goals are set, pursued, achieved, and celebrated. Additionally, there have been multiple global social and technological disruptions that have advanced the ways that we collect and analyze data, and that impact productivity, so the topic of goals and how to best accomplish them is ripe for disruption.

The BRIDGE methodology is a series of prompts that are designed to walk a user through the creation and execution of a personalized goal strategy that is science-based but that allows users to personalize each step for their own mindset, strengths, assets, support systems, and culture. This is cutting-edge and is designed to bring the best and most recent academic research on creating success to the mass market with a comprehensive framework that will help you establish a viable success plan.

Following are the questions in the six BRIDGE areas that must be addressed when seeking a goal outcome. Thinking them through will prepare you for your best chance of success. Each section will give you an example of the types of prompts you should consider, and book chapters devoted to each topic will lead you even deeper into helpful insights around key action steps to take.

BRAINSTORMING

Is this a learning or performance goal for me and my team? Who has accomplished this goal before and who does it best? If it's brand new, what are the areas that offer useful analogies or skills I can learn from? Are there new technologies or breakthroughs that will require me to update the ways I perform my checklist approach on performance goals? Am I brainstorming in an environment that will help me think outside of the box – for example, is there enough diversity of opinion and psychological safety in the group?

RELATIONSHIPS

Who do I need to go with me on this journey? Do I have the right team of people around me? If not, who do I need to add or meet? Where will I find them? Who should be dropped from my life during this goal pursuit? Who supports me at home and at work?

INVESTMENTS

What types of time, money, and energy do I need to invest to pursue and achieve this goal? Do I have access to them? How will my character strengths help me to succeed? How can I avoid the overuse of my strengths so that they don't become weaknesses? For example, do I have to go back to school or take a micro course to add a skill I lack? How quickly can I flatten my learning curve if I have a learning goal and invest in the right people, learning, and resources?

DECISION-MAKING

When I have made my best decisions, what have been the situations and their common denominators? When will it be time to act and what would be the signal that I need to back off or abort a course I'm on? Am I impacted by noise or bias in my decision-making and have I taken steps to identify when I'm most prone to make those mistakes and prevent them from entering my process?

GOOD GRIT

Do I have what it takes to do the hardest things required of me? What must I do to shore up my passion, persistence, and sense of purpose to succeed? For example, do I need more visible vision boards or motivational primes? Morning meditation sessions to build resilience? Changing my eating or drinking habits to improve self-regulation? Do I live in or have access to a contagious environment of grit that will enhance my efforts, but not result in stupid grit, selfie grit, or faux grit?

EXCELLENCE

How am I defining an excellent outcome? When is "good enough" an acceptable outcome that will keep me moving forward through the necessary steps toward success, and when will a different or enhanced kind of excellence be required? How will I measure my steps toward these outcomes? Will it be clear when I have achieved them?

How to Go from Here to There: Step-By-Step Worksheet for the BRIDGE Methodology

This worksheet might be best filled out after reading the book, answering the questions throughout the chapters, journaling, and taking notes as you assemble your best possible strategy. You can park some answers here as you go along and then come back to fill in the rest of the steps as you answer them, and you can do this over and over for all kinds of goals. Using goal setting theory as a foundation and adding the BRIDGE methodology on top with its comprehensive prompts is designed to help you create the "how" piece of what you will need to do to accomplish the goal. The more you do this, the more it will become second nature to you.

What's the goal? This could be a dream of yours, a sports goal, or even a KPI (key performance indicator) in a professional setting that is tied to an organization's OKR (objectives and key results). To ensure best outcomes in terms of fulfillment and positive change, make sure this is a goal you are choosing to pursue because it is important to you, or you understand its relevance and your role in a professional setting.

What meaningful change will occur as a result of accomplishing this goal? For individuals, this outcome could reinforce one's purpose in life, also known as *ikigai* in Japanese (that which I wake up for). These types of goals are "intrinsic" or self-motivated, and don't require external rewards.

Is this a performance goal or a learning goal? Bear in mind that it will be unusual to have a performance goal (something you've done before and you know the amount of effort and time it will take to achieve a specific outcome by a specific date) that doesn't have a touch of learning added, so factor in the possibility of small changes, regardless of how often you may have accomplished the same goal before.

◆ For a performance goal: Create a checklist of the steps involved in achieving this goal that could be an excellent guide for another person who is attempting the goal for the first time. Pilots have checklists, building contractors have checklists, hotel maids have checklists, surgeons have checklists, and people who want to guarantee an outcome that has been accomplished well by others all use checklists.

♦ For a learning goal: Write down what you need to learn to succeed at this goal. Example: You are a hostess at a busy restaurant, and you've never performed the types of duties that accompany this role. Your learning might include getting to know the layout of the restaurant and the table numbering system, learning the speed of different servers, and even how to deal with disruptive customers.

Brainstorm how you plan to accomplish the goal. Use out-of-the-box questions to come up with new ways of conceptualizing the goal. Be careful about how you brainstorm with others, and if you do, make sure to include people who are supportive of you and your goals to avoid comments that might discourage or derail you, even if they challenge you to look at your goal in new ways.

Detail the relationships that will be involved in the pursuit of your goal. Who will join you in this journey? Who should not be around you, or whose presence should be minimized because of their comments or behaviors? Who do you need to meet who could mentor or sponsor you, or give you advice or coaching?

What will you need to invest in in order to pursue this goal? Will you need to spend money on training, online courses, or returning to school? Will you need to invest time in becoming mentally prepared for taking action and changing your life? Will you have to deepen your relationships with proactive, positive people by deliberately spending more time in certain situations? Will you need to learn new coping skills that will shore up your resilience, like mindfulness? Will you need to acquire new language or technology skills?

How will you make the right decisions to support your goal pursuit? What types of risks will you need to take to move forward, and how will you become comfortable with any uncertainty or fear that arises? Do you know when you make your best and worst decisions and how to create or identify the conditions that accompany those situations? How will you decide to pivot from your plan, if necessary, and whether or not you should abort your actions because a situation has changed unexpectedly? Do you have a trusted set of advisors and friends whose feedback is essential to your strategy?

Do you have enough grit – passion, persistence, and purpose – to remain committed when the going is hard? Grit is an essential quality for challenging goals, and you will need will-power, a resilient mindset, and self-efficacy, among other qualities and behaviors. Do you have a plan for what you will say to yourself and do when obstacles emerge? Do you know how to avoid stupid grit, selfie grit, and faux grit?

What is the excellence you aim to achieve? What definition of excellence will let you know you are making the necessary progress toward your goal? What is the timeline to achieve your best outcome?

Premeditatio Malorum and *Premeditatio Bonum* Worksheet

Objective: Prepare for both potential obstacles and positive outcomes in goal pursuit.

- Goal Description: Clearly define the goal you are pursuing.
- Potential Obstacles: List possible challenges and negative scenarios (*premeditatio malorum*).
- Mitigation Strategies: Develop strategies to overcome each listed obstacle. How will you use your top strengths to do this? Are there new, creative ways you can apply your strengths in these efforts?
- Potential Positive Outcomes: List possible positive scenarios and opportunities (*premeditatio bonum*).
- Enhancement Strategies: Develop strategies to maximize your chances of positive outcomes. How will you use your top strengths to amplify these positive outcomes? Is there a new way you can combine several of your top strengths, or take a top strength and a lesser strength to make these best possible outcomes occur?

Black Swan Preparation Worksheet

Objective: Prepare for rare and unpredictable events that could impact goal achievement.

- ◆ Black Swan Scenarios: List potential black swan events that could affect your goal.
- ◆ Impact Analysis: Analyze the potential impact of each event.
- ◆ Contingency Plans: Develop contingency plans for each scenario.
- ◆ Reflection: Reflect on how being prepared for black swan events affects your confidence and planning.

Future Self Continuity Worksheet

Objective: Strengthen the connection between your present and future self.

- Letter to Future Self: Write a letter to yourself one year in the future (if you'd like to stretch yourself and it doesn't create anxiety, make the letter for 5 or 10 years in the future), reflecting on your accomplishments, who helped you with those accomplishments, what you are proudest of in that journey, and how the process of achieving your goals amplified important qualities like self-efficacy, self-confidence, gratitude, humility, and zest (jot down important points for this exercise on this worksheet and then write a full letter in a journal or other private place).
- Letter from Future Self: Write a letter from your future self to your present self, offering specific advice and encouragement.
- Reflection: Reflect on how this exercise influences your motivation and actions. Does this change anything about your current plan of action? What surprised you about this exercise because of its different perspective on thinking about the future from two different time periods?

Personal and Cultural Relevance Worksheet

Objective: Ensure that your goals and strategies are relevant to your personal and cultural context.

- ◆ Personal Relevance: Reflect on how your goals align with your personal values and circumstances.
- ◆ Cultural Relevance: Consider how your cultural background may influence your approach to your goals.
- ◆ Feedback: Seek feedback from individuals with similar backgrounds and experiences that will help you prepare for and overcome obstacles that are unique to your situation. Where will you find them? Try to get at least three different perspectives. Write below what you learn from these conversations and research.
- ◆ Adjustments: Make necessary adjustments to your goals and strategies based on this feedback and reflection on what you have learned.

First Principles Brainstorming Worksheet

Introduction: First Principles Thinking has its roots in ancient philosophy and has been developed and utilized across centuries in various fields, from philosophy to modern technological and business innovations, most recently popularized by Elon Musk, CEO of Tesla, SpaceX, and X. It's a powerful tool for critical thinking and problem-solving, enabling individuals and organizations to break free from traditional strategy exercises and think more innovatively.

Definition: Popularized by Aristotle and other Greek philosophers, First Principles Thinking involves breaking down complex problems into their most basic, foundational elements. It's about starting from scratch and questioning assumptions.

Section 1: Identify Your Goal/Dream

What do you want to achieve and why is it important to you?

Section 2: Challenge Assumptions

List the common assumptions or "standard practices" related to your goal. Challenge these assumptions.

Example: If your goal is to start a business, an assumption might be that you need a lot of capital to get started.

Section 3: Break Down the Goal

Break down your goal into its fundamental elements. What is absolutely necessary and what is not?

Using the fundamental elements you've identified, brainstorm new ways to achieve your goal. Be innovative and think outside the box.

Sample Brainstorming Questions (Modify for individuals or groups as needed)

1. **Reverse Thinking:** "If we were trying to achieve the opposite of our goal, what would we do differently? How can we apply this reversed thinking to our actual goal?"

2. **Historical Inspiration:** "How would a famous historical figure (like Leonardo da Vinci or Marie Curie) approach this goal? What unique insights or methods might they suggest?"

3. **Nature's Wisdom:** "What patterns or solutions in nature can inspire a new approach to our goal? For example, how does a spider's web or a beehive's structure inform our strategy?"

4. **Child's Perspective:** "How would a child approach this goal? What simple, imaginative solutions might they suggest that we have not considered?"

5. **Extraterrestrial Advice:** "If an intelligent alien civilization offered advice on our goal, what unconventional wisdom might they provide based on their unique perspective?"

6. **Cross-Industry Solutions:** "What solutions have been effective in completely different industries or fields that we can adapt to our own goal?"

7. **Limitation as an Asset:** "If we had half the resources or time, how would we approach our goal differently? How can this limitation breed creativity?"

8. **Futuristic Forecast:** "Imagine it's 50 years in the future. How would future technologies or societal changes make achieving our goal easier, and how can we simulate these conditions now?"

9. **Artistic Interpretation:** "How would an artist (painter, musician, writer) conceptualize our goal? Can their creative processes inspire a new approach?"

10. **Role Reversal:** "If our competitors or adversaries were in charge of achieving our goal, how would they go about it? What can we learn from this role reversal?"

11. **Time Travel Inquiry:** "If you could travel back in time, what advice would you give your past self about approaching this goal? Conversely, what might your future self, having already achieved it, advise you now?"

12. **Unexpected Collaboration:** "Which unexpected partner or industry could we collaborate with to bring a fresh perspective or new resources to our goal?"

13. **Cultural Shift:** "How would this goal be approached in a culture vastly different from ours? What unique practices or viewpoints could we adopt from them?"

14. **Science Fiction Scenario:** "How would this goal be achieved in a science fiction world? What imaginary technologies or social structures might make it easier?"

15. **Element of Play:** "How can we introduce elements of play or gamification into achieving our goal? What if it were a game with points, levels, or rewards?"

16. **Minimalist Approach:** "If we could only use the simplest, most basic tools and processes, how would we achieve our goal? What does this stripped-down approach reveal?"

17. **Random Connection:** "Pick a random object or concept and find a way to connect it to our goal. How does this unusual connection spark new ideas?"

18. **Analogies from Literature:** "What analogies can we draw from our favorite books or movies that might offer a novel perspective or solution?"

19. **Dream Logic:** "If you dreamt about achieving this goal, what strange or surreal elements might appear in the dream, and how could they be translated into realistic ideas?"

20. **The Impossible Question:** "What would we do if our goal was suddenly 10 times more ambitious? How would scaling up change our approach?"

21. **Alternate Reality Game:** "If our goal was the central mission of an alternate reality game, how would players go about solving it? What creative clues and challenges would they face?"

22. **Silent Brainstorming:** "If we had to brainstorm without speaking, using only visuals or written words, what new ideas might emerge from this form of communication?"

23. **Role of Technology:** "If we had access to a futuristic technology that does not exist yet, how would it change our approach to this goal? Can we simulate its effects with current technology?"

24. **Mythical Methodology:** "How would a character from mythology or folklore approach our goal? What ancient wisdom or mythical powers would they use?"

25. **Music-Inspired Strategy:** "If our goal could be represented by a genre of music, which one would it be and why? How can the characteristics of this music inspire our approach?"

26. **Interdisciplinary Connections:** "What can we learn from seemingly unrelated fields like astronomy, psychology, or culinary arts that could be applied to our goal?"

27. **Philosophical Perspectives:** "How would a famous philosopher approach our goal? What ethical or moral considerations might they bring to the forefront?"

28. **Color Theory Approach:** "If our goal could be represented by a color, which one would it be and why? How can the psychology of this color influence our strategy?"

29. **Embracing Failure:** "If we knew we could not fail, what bold or risky steps would we take toward our goal? Conversely, what can we learn from imagining a scenario where we fail spectacularly?"

30. **Wild Card Scenario:** "Introduce a 'wild card' – an unexpected event or change – into our planning. How would we adapt our strategy in response to this sudden shift?"

Heliotropic vs. Black Hole Worksheet

Objective: Identify and enhance relationships that evoke positive feelings and growth and the ones that have the opposite effect. These are also known as "catalysts" and "nurturers" in Teresa Amabile and Steven Kramer's "Progress Principle" research.

- ◆ Positive Interactions: List people who make you feel more positive and hopeful.
- ◆ Negative Interactions: List people who make you feel sad, pessimistic, tired, or demotivated.
- ◆ Reflection: Reflect on how these interactions affect your motivation and goal pursuit.
- ◆ Action Plan: Plan how to increase time spent with these positive individuals and less time with the negative ones.

Mind Mapping Relationships Worksheet

Objective: Create a mind map of relationships that will help you achieve your goals.

- ◆ Central Goal: Write your central goal (or a year of goals) in the middle of the page and draw a circle around it. Draw spokes off the goal that lead to the different goals or different sub-goals, depending on the map's intent.
- ◆ Key Relationships: List the key individuals or groups who can help you achieve your goal and add them to the mind map.
- ◆ Action Plan: Write down specific strategies – dates, places, mutual relationships, etc. – to engage with these key relationships and leverage their support.

Social Contagion Worksheet

Objective: Understand and manage the impact of social contagion on your behaviors and attitudes.

- ◆ Positive Behaviors: List positive behaviors or attitudes you want to reinforce. Who do you know who exhibits those behaviors and who would be a good influence for this exercise?
- ◆ Negative Behaviors: List negative behaviors or attitudes you want to avoid. Who in your life exhibits those behaviors?
- ◆ Action Plan: Develop strategies to spend more time with individuals who exhibit positive behaviors and less time with those who exhibit negative behaviors. Be specific.

Investment Inventory Worksheet

Objective: Identify and evaluate the necessary investments for achieving your goals.

- Goal Description: Clearly define your goal.
- Time Investments: List activities that will require significant time commitment.
- Financial Investments: Identify what financial resources will be needed, including courses, equipment, and professional services.
- Energy Investments: Describe the mental and physical energy that will be required for various tasks.
- Other Resources: Note additional resources such as mentors, support networks, and tools that will require investments of different kinds from you.

Resource Utilization Worksheet

Objective: Identify and utilize available resources effectively.

◆ Available Resources: List resources that are available to you, such as company programs, community services, or online tools.
◆ Resource Plan: Develop a plan for how you will utilize these resources.
◆ Resource Gaps: Identify any gaps in the resources you could benefit from and a plan for how to address them.

Reflection: Assess how effectively you are utilizing resources and make any adjustments as needed.

Balance and Trade-offs Worksheet

Objective: Manage trade-offs and balance different aspects of your life while pursuing your goals.

- ◆ Trade-offs: Identify trade-offs you will need to make to achieve your goal and how you will reallocate your resources to match your goal pursuit. For example, if you will be allocating time and money to learn a new trade, what will you need to give up?
- ◆ Balance Strategies: Write specific strategies to maintain balance in different areas of your life, with the understanding that pursuing big goals may mean a lack of balance from time to time.
- ◆ Reflection: Reflect on how well you are managing trade-offs and maintaining balance, and adjust as needed.

Game Theory in Decision-Making

Game theory is a branch of mathematics and economics that studies the strategic interactions between different players in a situation where their outcomes depend not only on their own actions, but also on the actions of other players. It's often used to analyze situations in economics, political science, biology, engineering, and even social interactions. Here's a brief overview of how it works and how it can be applied to decision-making for an average person:

UNDERSTANDING GAME THEORY

Basic Concepts: Game theory involves players (the decision-makers), strategies (the choices available to each player), and payoffs (the outcomes resulting from the combination of different strategies).

Types of Games

Zero-Sum Games

- **Definition:** Games where one player's gain is exactly balanced by the losses of other players
- **Example:** Chess, where one player's victory means the other player's defeat

Non-Zero-Sum Games

- **Definition:** Games where players' gains and losses are not always exactly balanced, allowing for cooperative strategies
- **Example:** Business negotiations, where both parties can potentially benefit

Key Strategies and Concepts

Nash Equilibrium

- **Definition:** A situation where no player can benefit by changing their strategy while the other players keep their strategies unchanged
- **Application:** Used to predict outcomes in competitive situations

Repeated Games

- **Definition:** Games involving players interacting over multiple rounds

◆ **Strategies:** Allows for the development of complex strategies like cooperation or punishment
◆ **Example:** The Prisoner's Dilemma played multiple times, where players can learn from past interactions

Application in Everyday Decision-Making

1. **Negotiation and Bargaining:** Understanding game theory can help in situations like salary negotiations, where you must anticipate the employer's responses to your demands.
2. **Making Choices in Social Dilemmas:** For example, in situations like the "Prisoner's Dilemma," game theory can help you understand the benefits and drawbacks of cooperative versus selfish behaviors.
3. **Understanding Competitive Situations:** In business or sports, game theory can guide decisions by analyzing how competitors are likely to act.
4. **Managing Risk and Uncertainty:** Game theory can help in making decisions under uncertainty by evaluating the probable outcomes of different choices.
5. **Long-term Strategy Planning:** Understanding repeated games can aid in developing long-term strategies in relationships, business, or politics by considering the future consequences of current actions.

Practical Tips for the Average Person

1. **Think Ahead and Reason Backward:** Anticipate others' responses to your actions and plan accordingly.
2. **Identify Incentives:** Understand what motivates other parties in an interaction.
3. **Recognize Patterns:** In repeated interactions, observe patterns and adjust your strategy.
4. **Cooperate When Appropriate:** In many real-life situations, cooperative strategies lead to better outcomes for all involved.
5. **Stay Informed and Rational:** Make decisions based on rational analysis rather than emotions.

Examples of Optimal Outcomes Using Game Theory

Example 1. Negotiating a Purchase or Salary

Situation: You're negotiating the price of a car or your salary.

Game Theory Application:

- **Understand the Seller's or Employer's Perspective:** Recognize their constraints and incentives. For a car dealer, the end of the month might be when they're more willing to negotiate to meet sales targets. For an employer, understanding their budget and the value of your skills can guide your salary negotiation.
- **Best Response Strategy:** Suggest a salary slightly higher than what you're willing to accept, expecting the other party to negotiate down, and do the opposite for a car.
- **Nash Equilibrium:** You reach a price or salary where neither you nor the dealer/employer has an incentive to deviate from the agreed amount, considering the circumstances.

Optimal Outcome: You secure a deal closer to your ideal price or salary, and the other party also feels satisfied with the agreement.

Example 2. Participating in a Group Project or Work Team

Situation: You are part of a team working on a project with shared responsibility and credit.

Game Theory Application

- **Prisoner's Dilemma:** Each team member can choose to work hard (cooperate) or slack off (defect). If everyone cooperates, the project succeeds. If too many defect, the project fails.
- **Iterated Game:** Since you might work with these people again, your current actions will influence future interactions.

◆ **Tit-for-Tat Strategy:** Start by cooperating (working hard), then mimic your teammates' previous actions in future projects. If they work hard, you do the same; if they slack off, you adjust your effort accordingly.

Optimal Outcome: Promotes a cooperative environment. Team members are more likely to contribute effectively, knowing that their efforts will be matched and reciprocated.

Example 3. Making Decisions in Shared Resources or Public Goods

Situation: Deciding whether to contribute to a public good, like a community garden or a neighborhood watch program.

Game Theory Application

◆ **Tragedy of the Commons:** If everyone acts in their self-interest (not contributing to the public good), the resource is depleted or the project fails.
◆ **Communicate and Establish Norms:** By discussing and agreeing on fair contributions (time, money, effort), you can encourage participation.
◆ **Repeated Interactions:** In a community, repeated interactions mean your choices will affect your reputation and future cooperation from neighbors.

Optimal Outcome: Ensures the sustainability of the public good. By contributing and encouraging others to do so, the community benefits from the shared resource or initiative.

In each of these examples, game theory helps in understanding and predicting the behavior of others, guiding you toward a strategy that leads to a mutually beneficial outcome. So, while game theory might seem abstract, its principles can be applied to everyday decision-making, helping individuals to better analyze and anticipate the actions of others in various situations, which is valuable knowledge for creating strategies to effectively maximize your chances of goal achievement.

Overcoming Procrastination Worksheet

Objective: Identify and overcome procrastination tendencies.

- Procrastination Triggers: Identify triggers that lead to procrastination.
- Anticipation of Hassle: Reflect on how anticipating a hassle affects your goal pursuit.
- Overcoming Strategies: Develop strategies to overcome procrastination and get started on tasks.
- Action Plan: Create a detailed plan to tackle tasks and avoid procrastination.
- Reflection: Reflect on your progress and make adjustments as needed.

Decision-Making Framework Worksheet

Objective: Establish a structured approach to making important decisions.

- Decision Description: Clearly define the decision to be made.
- Options: List all possible options or courses of action.
- Criteria: Establish criteria for evaluating each option.
- Analysis: Analyze each option based on the established criteria.
- Decision: Make a final decision based on the analysis.
- Reflection: Reflect on the decision-making process and outcomes.

Decision Audit Worksheet

Objective: Conduct an audit of past decisions to improve future decision-making.

- Decision Summary: Summarize the decision made.
- Outcome: Describe the outcome of the decision.
- Successes: Identify what went well in the decision-making process.
- Failures: Identify what went wrong or could have been improved.
- Lessons Learned: List lessons learned from the decision.
- Future Improvements: Develop strategies for improving future decision-making.

Decision-Making Checklist

Objective: Create a checklist to guide consistent and effective decision-making.

- Decision Steps: List the steps in the decision-making process (five to seven steps are recommended for checklists because of how our brains operate and remember lists).
- Key Considerations: Identify key considerations for each step.
- Verification: Write how you will ensure all steps and considerations have been addressed. Will the list be posted publicly? Will someone or a team hold you accountable?
- Reflection: Reflect on the use of the checklist and its effectiveness after it has been tested several times. Ask others who have accomplished the same goal if they understand and can follow your checklist. Is there anything that can be improved or changed?

Bias and Noise Awareness Worksheet

Objective: Identify and mitigate biases and noise in decision-making.

- Bias Identification: List potential biases that could affect your decision.
- Noise Identification: Identify sources of noise that could impact your judgment.
- Mitigation Strategies: Develop strategies to reduce bias and noise.
- Reflection: Reflect on how biases and noise were managed and their impact on the decision.

Grit Development Worksheet

Objective: Cultivate and strengthen your grit through specific strategies and reflections.

Current Grit Assessment:

- Take the Grit Scale test to assess your current level of grit at https://angeladuckworth.com/grit-scale.
- Reflect on your scores and identify areas for improvement.

Passion and Perseverance:

- Identify a challenging long-term goal you are passionate about.
- List specific actions to maintain and increase your passion for this goal.
- Outline strategies to enhance perseverance when faced with obstacles.

Purpose:

- Identify the "why" behind this goal to ensure that this is a goal that is meaningful to you, and not necessarily anyone else. Another question you can ask is "So what?" So what if you accomplish this goal? Why is it meaningful to you and what will change or be different if you achieve the goal? Who else will benefit from the accomplishment of the goal? Will it detract from anyone else's well-being or will it enhance others' lives?

Support System:

- Identify key individuals who can support your journey.
- Develop a plan to engage with and leverage their support.

Action Plan:

- Set milestones and track your progress toward the goal.
- Reflect on your journey regularly and adjust your plan as needed.

Good Grit versus Bad Grit Worksheet

Objective: Differentiate between good grit and bad grit and apply this understanding to your goals.

- ◆ Definitions: Define good grit (authentic grit that has the potential to awe and inspire others because of how the goal is pursued, thus uplifting others) and bad grit (stupid grit, selfie grit, or faux grit).
- ◆ Personal Examples: Reflect on times when you or others exhibited good grit and bad grit that either inspired or repelled you.
- ◆ Impact Analysis: Analyze the impact of good grit and bad grit on your goals and relationships.
- ◆ Action Plan: Develop a plan to cultivate good grit and avoid bad grit in your goal pursuit.

Relational Grit Worksheet

Objective: Strengthen relationships that support and enhance your grit.
   Identify Key Relationships:

- List individuals who provide positive support and encouragement, and whose input and interactions with you make you believe you can do hard things – particularly things you have never done before. Are there common threads connecting these people?
- Describe how these relationships specifically impact your cultivation and ability to exhibit good grit in goal pursuit.
- What are your specific strategies to nurture and strengthen these relationships? Will you seek them out more frequently? Will you share your goals with them and ask for help or advice?
- List the people who build and amplify relational grit because of how you interact with them. Are there common threads among how you know them?

Excellence Definition Worksheet

Objective: Define what excellence means to you and align your actions and goals with this definition.

Personal Definition of Excellence:

◆ How do you define excellence in your personal and professional life?
◆ What are the key characteristics of this definition?

Role Models and Inspirations:

◆ Who are your role models for excellence and what did they accomplish?
◆ What qualities do they exhibit that you admire?

Excellence in Action:

◆ Describe actions or behaviors that align with your definition of excellence.
◆ How will you incorporate these types of actions into your daily routine?

Reflection:

◆ Reflect on situations where you achieved excellence.
◆ How did it feel, and what impact did it have on your future goals?
◆ Did others give you feedback about how your excellence impacted them? If yes, describe.

Authentic Pride versus Hubristic Pride Worksheet

Objective: Describe authentic and hubristic pride. What are the key differences between them?

Understanding Authentic Pride:

- Define authentic pride.
- List characteristics of authentic pride (e.g. humility, gratitude).
- List people who have this quality and what you observed about them.

Understanding Hubristic Pride:

- Define hubristic pride.
- List characteristics of hubristic pride (e.g., arrogance, narcissism).
- List people who have this quality and what you observed about them.

Personal Reflection:

- Reflect on a time when you felt authentic pride. What were the circumstances, and what did you achieve?
- Reflect on a time when you felt hubristic pride. What were the circumstances, and how did it affect you?

Cultivating Authentic Pride:

- Identify actions and behaviors that will help you cultivate authentic pride.
- Develop a plan to avoid falling into hubristic pride.

Acknowledgments

Writing a book is like giving birth, and bringing this one to life was a journey of collaboration and support. From an exploratory conversation to publication in under a year, this book's creation broke new personal records for speed without sacrificing excellence.

First and foremost, my heartfelt gratitude goes to Anne Bruce, whose generosity toward a fellow author she'd never met was a beacon of support. It was Anne who suggested Cheryl Segura at Wiley acquire this book, which had been brewing inside me for years. Thanks to my wonderful agent, Ivor Whitson, and his amazing wife, Ronnie, the deal was swiftly sealed after just two phone calls and a few emails. I was also fortunate to have Kelly Talbot bring skill and kindness to the editing process, adding the finishing touches that made all the difference.

A special thank you to my team of incredible women warriors who kept everything running smoothly behind the scenes while I immersed myself in the research and writing of this book at Capital Workspaces, my co-working home in Bethesda, MD. Talia Schatzman, my social media head; Melissa Spencer, my speaker manager; and Debbie Mahony of DesignSpinner, my talented website designer – your support was invaluable.

A special shout out to "Hero Effect" speaker Kevin Brown, whose brainstorming session years ago led to the "BRIDGE" acronym – a stroke of inspiration that came to him in his sleep. It stuck. My deep appreciation also goes to the brilliant visionary Brian Johnson, Founder and CEO of Heroic, who enthusiastically agreed to write the Foreword and who introduced me to his passionate global followers.

Gary Latham, co-founder of Goal Setting Theory, has been a steadfast supporter of my work for nearly 20 years. His endorsement of this book is a cherished gift. And a special thank you to the legions of researchers and academics who do rigorous scholarship in labs and universities all over the world, but whose names may be unfamiliar to the general public because they don't have the time or desire to translate their findings into mass market books. Your work matters, and I couldn't have written this book without the benefit of the research you do.

I am profoundly grateful to Paul Thomas, Soroor Mohammad, and Olena Levanda, who have kept me healthy, happy, and flourishing in body, mind, and soul for 30 years.

My two Mastermind groups have been vital sounding boards and cheerleaders over many years. Thank you to Louisa Jewell, Elaine O'Brien, and Margarita Tarragona in my longest-lived group, and to Erin Dullea, Tamara Myles, and Jan Stanley in the "Tall Poppies" group.

To my children and their partners, Haywood Miller IV and Abbey Bonyata, Samantha and Joey Kavanagh, and Bayard and Lily Miller – your ideas, stories, and feedback were invaluable. You also noted that I handled the stress of my ninth book's deadlines better than I'd handled book deadlines before, proving that deliberate practice makes perfect!

And to my husband, Haywood Miller III, who took on the task of walking our giant schnoodle, Alpha, alone for five months and who kept restaurants and bartenders entertained across Rehoboth Beach, DE: your support, love, and pride in what I do provided the blocks of alone time that every author for all time has always needed for inspiration, creation, and finishing what they start.

Finally, thank you to everyone who believed in me and the importance of this book. I hope it brings optimism and zest to readers all over the world that will make everyone's big goals easier to accomplish, and as a result, may future generations draw upon more stories of role models who will now decide to do hard things with proven tools after reading this book.

About the Author

Caroline Adams Miller is the author of nine bestselling books, including *My Name Is Caroline*, *Creating Your Best Life*, and *Getting Grit*, which have been translated into multiple languages. The "father of Positive Psychology," Dr. Martin Seligman, wrote about Caroline's unique ability to mesh the science of happiness with the science of success in his book, *Flourish*, noting that she "added a major missing piece" to the scholarship of coaching people to flourish and achieve their goals in her fifth book, *Creating Your Best Life*. Dr. Angela Duckworth, whose research on grit led to a MacArthur Genius grant, said about *Getting Grit*, "No one has thought more than Caroline about how to apply the scientific research on grit and achievement to our own lives!"

Creating Your Best Life was the first evidence-based mass market book to bring the science of success and Locke and Latham's goal setting theory together with the research on happiness, leading it to be ranked #1 on goal setting lists for more than 10 years because of its rigorous blend of theory with practical solutions for change. *Getting Grit* was listed as one of the "top ten books that will change your life" in 2017 and as one of the "top 25 books that will help you find your purpose" in 2023.

Miller's first book, *My Name Is Caroline*, broke the silence around bulimia in 1988 by being the first autobiographical book on successful recovery, which she followed up with *Positively Caroline* in 2013 about how she had maintained unbroken recovery from her eating disorder for more than 30 years. Her pioneering courage in telling her story to provide hope at a time when there was no known treatment has been cited by many professionals as a turning point that broke the stigma and shame many people feel about suffering from an eating disorder.

Miller is frequently featured in the media as an expert on how to achieve hard goals and thrive, and her TEDx talk on "The Moments

That Make Champions" has garnered tens of thousands of views. she has taught in many schools and universities, including as an adjunct lecturer in the Wharton Executive Education program, and she keynotes and leads workshops all over the world on goals, grit, and happiness. Miller is a professional executive coach who works with global CEOs and leaders from many industries, many of whom fly to her retreat center in Rehoboth Beach, Delaware every year to refine their evidence-based goal setting approaches and learn how to integrate her BRIDGE methodology into their strategy.

Miller is one of the first 32 people to attain a Masters of Positive Psychology (MAPP) from the University of Pennsylvania and she graduated *magna cum laude* from Harvard University. She is a black belt martial artist and Masters swimmer with three adult children, and she splits her time between Bethesda, Maryland and Rehoboth Beach, Delaware with her husband, Haywood.

Index